THE U.S.
IMMIGRATION
CRISIS

CASCADE COMPANIONS

The Christian theological tradition provides an embarrassment of riches: from Scripture to modern scholarship, we are blessed with a vast and complex theological inheritance. And yet this feast of traditional riches is too frequently inaccessible to the general reader.

The Cascade Companions series addresses the challenge by publishing books that combine academic rigor with broad appeal and readability. They aim to introduce nonspecialist readers to that vital storehouse of authors, documents, themes, histories, arguments, and movements that comprise this heritage with brief yet compelling volumes.

THE U.S. IMMIGRATION CRISIS

Toward an Ethics of Place

MIGUEL A. DE LA TORRE

 CASCADE *Books* • Eugene, Oregon

THE U.S. IMMIGRATION CRISIS
Toward an Ethics of Place

Cascade Companions

Cascade Books
An Imprint of Wipf and Stock Publishers
199 W. 8th Ave., Suite 3
Eugene, OR 97401

www.wipfandstock.com

PAPERBACK ISBN 13: 978-1-4982-2369-0
HARDCOVER ISBN 13: 978-1-4982-2371-3
ELECTRONIC ISBN 13: 978-1-4982-2370-6

Cataloguing-in-Publication data:

Names: De La Torre, Miguel A.
Title: The U.S. immigration crisis : toward an ethics of place / Miguel
    A. De La Torre.
Description: Eugene, OR : Cascade Books, 2016 | Cascade Compan-
    ions | Includes bibliographical references and index.
Identifiers: ISBN 978-1-4982-2369-0 (paperback) | ISBN 978-1-4982-
    2371-3 (hardcover) | ISBN 978-1-4982-2370-6 (ebook)
Subjects: LCSH: Emigration and immigration—Moral and ethical
    aspects. | United States—Emigration and immigration.
Classification: LCC JV6477 D35 2016 (print) | LCC JV6477 (ebook)

Manufactured in the U.S.A.   06/10/2016

Dedicated to:
BorderLinks
Humane Borders
No More Deaths
Samaritans
Southside Presbyterian Church
. . . and the hundreds of activists, churches, and
organizations that occupy space on the borders
between privilege and dispossession,
accompanying the disenfranchised

CONTENTS

THE NEW COLOSSUS

Not like the brazen giant of Greek fame,
With conquering limbs astride from land to land;
Here at our sea-washed, sunset gates shall stand
A mighty woman with a torch, whose flame
Is the imprisoned lightning, and her name
Mother of Exiles. From her beacon-hand
Glows world-wide welcome; her mild eyes command
The air-bridged harbor that twin cities frame.
"Keep ancient lands, your storied pomp!" cries she
With silent lips. "Give me your tired, your poor,
Your huddled masses yearning to breathe free,
The wretched refuse of your teeming shore.
Send these, the homeless, tempest-tost to me,
I lift my lamp beside the golden door!"

—Poem by Emma Lazarus engraved on a tablet
within the pedestal on which the Statue of Liberty stands.

PREFACE

To PROTECT THE IDENTITY of the undocumented immigrant living on the underside of U.S. privilege, I never asked for their real names and instead asked them to assign themselves an alias. They bestowed upon me an awesome responsibility of reflecting on their testimonies and actions to ethically explain what they are doing and why it is being done. I am grateful for the confidence they have offered me. I am also cognizant of too many individuals who deserve a shout out, and to begin such a list would fill too many pages and, no doubt, overlook several key persons. So while I provide a generic thank you to all those who have allowed me to be present with them in their struggle, I would be remiss if I did not at least recognize three individuals who were always at the other end of a phone call or an email willing to answer my many questions, contributing to whatever success this book project might demonstrate. Specifically, I need to express my gratitude by recognizing John Fife, cofounder of No More Deaths; Fernanda Morillon, director of Borderlinks; and Alison Harrington, pastor of Southside Presbyterian Church.

INTRODUCTION

¡Presente!

A FEW YEARS AGO, I shared a not-yet-completed manuscript with my class of doctoral students in an effort to
receive feedback on some concepts I was developing surrounding the theme of indecent ethics. When I eventually
presented those thoughts at a conference, I discovered that
one of those students was passing off my work as their own,
without proper attribution. As could be imagined, I was
enraged. Some time passed before I began to realize that
there is nothing new under the sun. I was forced to deal
with my own arrogance that somehow my ideas were constructed *ex nihilo*, as if from some vacuum. No concept that
I can imagine, regardless as to how unique it may appear to
be, can be solely attributed to me. I have often heard many
colleagues state that they stand on the shoulders of those
scholars who came before them. But if I am honest with
myself, the shoulders upon whom I stand are mainly those
of the oppressed and the activists placing their bodies in the
same space for the cause of justice.

One of the foundational principles of those who
align themselves with liberative ethical thinking is that our

concepts are simply a reflection of what the marginalized and their allies are doing and saying. For some, this tenet is but rhetoric; but for me, I truly believe this with all my being. And if I really do, then I should not have been annoyed with my former student, for all of the ethical concepts that I and other liberative thinkers are constructing have already been developed by those on the margins of society. If our concepts have not arisen from the grassroots, then they really cannot be liberative because of their disconnect with the oppressed. The job of the scholar is to translate this grassroots praxis to a more general audience in an accessible matter (oblique writing does not equal brilliance) so as to raise the consciousness of society. We fail as academics (including those of us who are liberationists) because we treat the production of knowledge as private property.

Many of us in the academy have been highly influenced by the capitalist concept that commodifies even our thoughts, presenting recycled perspectives and ideas as if they have never before existed. And yet, for the true liberative thinker, there must be a move away from developing thoughts in the seclusion of our ivory towers toward recording the creative conversations already taking place on the streets located away from "good" neighborhoods by those who lack abbreviations after their names, and at times, lack even formal schooling. Could it be that a true liberative thinker is a plagiarist of what the disenfranchised are doing and saying? Not exactly. While it is crucial for scholars to maintain academic integrity and attribute thoughts and concepts to those who helped develop the conversation, I fear that all too often we are attributing the wrong people. We are quick to quote another scholar with academic credentials, and if we are honest, we just quote our academic friends while totally ignoring those scholars of whom we are jealous or simply don't like. But in our rush to fill a footnote, we often ignore the true source that launched our creative thinking, those from the margins of society.

So here is the true ethical dilemma for the scholar. At what point are we simply appropriating the stories of the oppressed and of the activists standing in solidarity with them for our own purposes, i.e. getting an article or book published, getting tenure or promotion, developing a reputation among our peers as an expert in the field? As Stacey Floyd-Thomas reminds us: If you are gong to appropriate, you have to reciprocate. In a postscript to womanist allies she writes, "The intentional and concomitant effort of others to participate in solidarity with and on behalf of Black women who have made available, shared, and translated their wisdom, strategies, and methods for the universal task of liberating the oppressed and speaking truth to power."[1]

What do I owe those on the margins when I tell their stories or use their concepts? A simple attribution or footnote is not enough. How do I use the benefits I received by appropriating their labor to then move our liberating task closer toward justice? If I don't reciprocate, then I become a plagiarist of the worst form (not that there exists any plagiarist of the best form!). To be a liberative thinker means that I too must accompany the oppressed in their struggle. I too must at times put down my pen and notepad and place my body in the same precarious space that they occupy. For only then can I do this thing we call scholarship with integrity. Just to be clear, every concept, thought, strategy, or idea I have ever developed should be attributed to the disenfranchised and the many who stand with them fighting for justice. Being grateful to them is not enough: I must learn to be *¡Presente!*

When I am present, I quickly discover that those on the margins of society are having a very different conversation

1. Floyd-Thomas, *Deeper Shades of Purple,* 250.

than those who simply rely on cable news programs for their information. For example, anyone can write or talk about the current immigration dilemma. Anyone can have an opinion. But how do we move beyond the sound bites dominating the conversation, moving instead to the difficult task of exploring the historical, economic, and social structures that conspire to create a crisis where millions of brown bodies suffer injury, incarceration, death, or if they are lucky to succeed, a lifetime of living in the shadows? Many articles, books, and news accounts focus on the plight of the undocumented, but few try to understand why they come. Many writings exist that present us with a description, rather than show how we can stand in solidarity with the undocumented and their allies, accompanying them in their struggle.

All too often, we do ethical analyses from the comfort of our cushy armchairs. From the safety of our academic departments we gaze at the misfortunes of the undocumented and paternalistically describe their dilemma, denying them subjectivity by making them the object of our discourse. It becomes easier to talk about them than listening and learning from their stories, their testimonies. This book is made possible because of the many undocumented immigrants who took a risk to chat with me about their experience. The actions these immigrants take so that their families can have life are inspiring. But so are the actions of their allies who chose to occupy the same space as the dispossessed to accompany them in their struggle for justice.

We normatively begin any ethical contemplation by establishing a theory that we claim as truth, maybe even universal truth. This theory can be based on our ability to reason, or on some sacred text, or on the teachings of the church, or even some government document (i.e., U.S. Constitution) that we consider inspired. Once this theory is designated as true, we determine what should be the correct action (as a second step to life) that needs to be implemented. We know what to do because we already determine what to believe; thus orthopraxis (*ortho*: correct, *praxis*: actions) flows from orthodoxy (*ortho*: correct, *doxos*: doctrine). Based on the truth of X, we should do Y. We see this methodology played out in almost every ethics class taught throughout the U.S. (and beyond) that employs case studies as a means of learning ethical analysis.

Eurocentric ethics is usually taught through hypothetical case studies where the student attempts to determine in what action to engage based on the theory already learned. The objective is not to engage in justice-based acts to confront the dilemma presented; rather, to determine "objectively," based on a multitude of possibilities, which ethical response is proper, which ethical response is in line with what we claim to believe. Such an approach to ethical analysis creates a false dichotomy between ethical theory and practice. The purpose ceases to be the determination of which moral actions to engage in the presence of injustice and oppression; but instead, the student is taught to answer some ethical abstract question that helps us think better about what ethics is or should be. I have argued that in spite of how clever or creative case studies may appear to be, they are useless to those residing on the margins of society because they fail to foster concrete acts that can bring about change. A spectator-type ethics is created where debating theory, rather than transforming society, becomes the ultimate intellectual goal. Ethics devoid of praxis may be philosophical or theological; but it is not ethics.

Those of us engaged in liberative ethics have strived to turn this methodology upon its head. We have argued for decades that theory, orthodoxy, flows from action, orthopraxis. Skeptical of universal truths or all-encompassing theories existing beyond the reach of finite minds, liberative ethicists argue that through justice-based actions geared to transform society, we can come *closer* to understanding what correct doctrine might look like. We lack the hubris to claim we arrived at truth; nevertheless, we can claim with confidence that the liberating praxis in which we engage has helped us come nearer to whatever truth (if it exists) might be. Justice-based praxis, engaged in transforming society, can help us to better understanding the spiritual.

But even liberative-minded scholars have fallen into the trap of claiming the importance of social location without being present, as if the exercise of thinking can lead to understanding, even if one's body is physically miles away, teaching in some classroom. A danger exists for us academics who present ourselves as experts, but fail to occupy the same space as the disenfranchised, the same location in where the object of our gaze resides. An ethics of place[2] recognizes that the physical location in which the oppressed reside is crucial in understanding which ethics, which praxis, needs to be engaged. Not to be *presente* questions the ability to truly understand the dilemma under investigation. Physically engaging in consciousness-raising

2. I am aware that scholars such as Mick Smith have used the term "an ethics of place" as a means by which to re-engage the moral and ethical concerns of radical ecological theories; that J. K. Gibson Graham uses the term "an ethics of the local" in a Marxist analysis grounded in the necessary failure of the global order; and that John Inge uses the term "a theology of place" to stress taking seriously the importance of place which contributes to the creation of the identity of community, and vice versa with both endangered by the effects of globalization responsible for the erosion of people's rootedness. I am using the phrase "an ethics of place" somewhat differently then how others have used the term. For me, an ethics of place means that praxis must be developed in the place of oppression, in the midst of the effects of institutionalized disenfranchisement in the hopes of creating an ethical response. When I use the term, ethics of place, I mean that ethical analysis, to be contextual, must also pay close attention to the physical local of the marginalized.

praxis leads to understanding the causes of oppression, from which a spiritual response flows that can lead to better informed theories or doctrines. In the doing of liberative acts (ethics), theory (theology) is formed as a reflection of praxis.

This book is an example of employing an ethics of place, recognizing that as an organic intellectual, I reflect on the praxis of those who are actually crossing deserts as a response to the injustices forced upon them and upon those who are documented who place their bodies on the line so as to be in solidarity with the dispossessed. My job as a scholar of ethics is to reflect upon the praxis in which those seeking justice, as and for immigrants, engage. I dishonor them when I try to fit their actions into some predetermined theory that neatly orders my worldview. Instead, I should seek to give voice and a language to what already is occurring—even when the voice given is as messy and contradictory as the actions they are taking. What I and my fellow liberative scholars do in the classroom is not praxis. After all, we get paid to do this in relative safety. This is not to dismiss or disregard what we do, for it is important work, helping to highlight issues that are usually lost in the static of the everyday; but we should never delude ourselves into thinking that somehow we are engaged by simply reflecting on what "those poor immigrants must go through."

An ethics of place insists that the scholar be present, to also occupy the space of the undocumented and their allies. Absence denies the scholar of any gravitas. Only when I am in the moment, seeing what they see, can I better understand in what actions to accompany them. How can I write about the immigration dilemma if I do not walk the migrant trails, or sit in court while they are being processed, or worship with them at the church where they are seeking sanctuary? If I refuse to be *presente*, I simply will be another clueless ignoramus who somehow believes that my academic credentials are all that is needed to know and understand their experience. An ethics of place is what makes me an ethicist, what provides gravitas to my voice, not because I am somehow smarter, but because I chose to learn from the undocumented and their documented allies.

Eurocentric ethicists may strive to understand the world; but because these scholars fail to be present, they all to often will lack the ability of differentiating between a blink and a wink.[3] Their efforts can only conclude with disappointing analysis that fails to resonate with those most disenfranchised. Then there are those who, as scholar-activists, are more concerned with changing the world toward a more just and liberative social order. This book attempts the latter strategy by placing the reader in the place of those struggling for immigration justice. The only hope that any ethicist can have of their work holding relevance among those who structurally are suffering is to be present, to radically be in solidarity with those on the margins. However we define ethics in the future, it should be derived from occupying the same physical space as the dispossessed.

This manuscript is possible not because I took time to write it, but because so many took time to stand in solidarity with the disenfranchised undocumented immigrant. Although it will be my expressed purpose to help the reader better grasp the complexity of the immigration dilemma by inviting them to join us in the place where oppression systematically and unnoticeably occurs, my ultimate goal is to invite the reader to leave their comfortable space and join the undocumented and their allies in the continued struggle for justice. In other words, to be *¡Presente!*

3. Geertz, "Thick Description," in *Interpretations of Culture,* 6.

1

ON A STREET CORNER IN NOGALES, MEXICO

ALONG A SUPERIMPOSED 1,833-MILE line, the richest and most powerful nation ever known to humanity is separated from what is derogatorily referred to as the Third World. The United States is not separated from its neighbors to the south by some natural boundary; instead, this border was artificially created, a direct consequence of the U.S. territorial conquest of northern Mexico (1846–48). To live on the physical international border is to live in a war zone, where the greatest military power ever known in history amasses against the supposed threat of poor brown people. Borderlands are not solely geographic locations; they are also social locations. Those living south of the border live separated from the benefits and fruits of their labor exported northward. This economic social structure of exclusion prevails because Mexicans and Central Americans—and by extension U.S. Latinxs[1]—are conceived by the dominant

1. Throught the book I have used the more generic term

Euroamerican culture as being inferior. They are perceived as inferior partly due to the pervasive race-conscious U.S. culture. For centuries Euroamericans have been taught to equate nonwhites, specifically mixed-race persons, as less-than. To be a "half-breed," a mixture of races and ethnicities (Caucasian, African, Indigenous, or any combination thereof) meant limited access to opportunities and social services. Not much has changed. To physically be in the social location of the borderlands' war zone is to recognize the fragility of brown life. And although brown lives *also* matter, they remain cheap and dispensable by those on the border with high-tech surveillance and weapons. Since the days of the Texas Rangers almost a century ago, when brown bodies were lynched for sport, to today where brown bodies are indiscriminatively shot, brown lives remain expendable.

On a balmy December day, I stand on a Nogales street corner in Mexico. Directly across the street is a white medical clinic with rusted bars on the windows and worn out protruding yellow signage that reads "*Emergencias Medicas*." Directly to my left is *Calle Internacional*, a two-lane street that runs along the perimeter of the wall, built to demarcate the international border existing between the United States and Mexico. This wall has not always existed. There was a time when the residents on both sides of this border town would travel across the international border to shop and work with minor hindrances. The genesis of the wall was 1994 (shortly after the ratification of NAFTA) when landing strips used during the First Iraqi War were recycled by Immigration and Naturalization Service (INS) to construct a wall in hopes of stemming the flow of mainly Mexican immigrants through Nogales and San Diego.

"Latinx(s)" where one might be more accustomed to seeing "Hispanic(s)" or "Latino/a(s)."

As I cross the street toward the corner clinic I immediately notice bullet holes on the façade. I count twelve, each encircled by a fading red mark. Along the clinic's northern wall facing the colossal international wall are plastered handbills of a teenager's face with the word "*¡JUSTICIA!*" embolden under the portrait. There is also a mural of the same boy with a halo jumping rope. A three-foot ornate white cross with an intertwining red rose leans against the clinic's wall with a picture of the same boy in its center. His name was José Antonio Elena Rodríguez, a teenager who aspired to one day join the Mexican military. Clearly he perished at this site in a hail of bullets. But why? Was he a gang-banger, or an innocent pedestrian caught up in some drug related drive-by shooting?

Photographer: Vincent De La Torre

The sixteen-year-old boy died with two shots to the head and eight shots to the back, just three blocks away from his home. Based on the autopsy report, he was facing away from his assailant. On the evening of October 10, 2012, José told his grandmother, Taide Elena, that he was going to visit his brother Diego, an Oxxo convenience store clerk, at work to help him lock up. The route to the Oxxo took him along *Calle Internacional*. José, whose father died three years earlier, was a studious boy; but due to financial difficulties, he was suspended from school when the family was unable to pay the tuition. He was, nonetheless, excited to be starting classes again in the next week. As José left home and began his walk toward *Calle Internacional*, on the other side of the wall, in a different world, border agents received a 911 call that men were hoisting bundles of marijuana over the wall, a common occurrence.

John Zuniga, a K-9 officer, was the first to arrive at the scene. He saw two men attempting to climb the wall back into Mexico. The agent claimed to have shouted at them to stop; even though at least three witnesses on the Mexican side confirmed they heard no shouts. Zuniga says that as soon as he shouted at the perpetrators, he heard rocks hitting the ground and saw several stones flying through the air. Zuniga returned to his vehicle to lock up his dog and take cover when he heard gunshots. Looking up, he saw fellow agent Lonnie Swartz firing into Mexico. According to Sonora state police ballistic reports, at least one agent fired fourteen hollow-point bullets from a standard issue .40-caliber Heckler & Koch pistol. This means that the agent must have emptied his revolver, reloaded, and kept on shooting. According to Isidro Alvarado, a security guard who was walking about twenty feet behind José, he saw two youths run past the lad, away from the wall. That's when he heard gunshots and saw José fall.[2]

I crossed *Calle Internacional* and past the vehicles parked on a 45-degree angle against a rock formation that is about twenty-five feet high. On top of this bluff is the wall, roughly eighteen feet tall. The once solid wall build from recycled landing strips was replaced in 2006 with circular steel bars, giving the impression of a jail locking brown bodies out, and in. Because of the distance from the clinic

2. Ortega and O'Dell, "Deadly Border Agent Incidents."

to the wall (about thirty feet), the height of the wall above the rock formation (about forty-three feet), and the arc that the rock would need to travel to make it over the wall, it is almost physically impossible for any rock to be thrown from the clinic and make its way to the U.S. side. Maybe a Major League baseball player could accomplish this herculean feat; but even then, it is doubtful that the missive thrown would do any harm.

Additionally, the agent would have had to be up against the wall to fire his weapon through the 3.5-inch gap between the steel bars. A rock would have had to violate the laws of physics, once it went over the wall, and instead of continuing in a downward arc, it would need to change direction and fall parallel with the wall to create any threat for the shooting officer. In theory, José could have thrown the rock through the 3.5 inch gaps, a challenging achievement at night. Also, because José was shot in the back, he would have had to throw the alleged rock over his shoulder. I notice the wall security camera just fifty yards from where José was killed facing the shot-up clinic façade. The images captured that evening could easily clear up the inconsistencies and incongruencies surrounding the event; but thus far, the Border Patrol has refused to release said video. The video can demonstrate if the Mexican witnesses are correct in asserting that José was not throwing rocks.

José Antonio Elena Rodríguez is not the only one to perish by Border Patrol agents while on Mexican soil. Sergio Adrian Hernandez-Guereca (age fifteen) was shot in Ciudad Juarez while accompanying his older brother Omar to work. While Omar did maintenance repairs on the Paso del Norte border bridge, Sergio, along with other boys played on the dry bed of the Rio Grande. He was shot by Border Patrol agent Jesús Mesa Jr. when he peeked from behind a column where he sought cover. The agent fired at

Sergio while twelve yards from the border on the U.S. side. Mesa claimed he was surrounded by rock throwing youth, and fearing for his life acted in self-defense. But when several cell phone videos surfaced capturing the incident, Mesa's version of what occurred proved to be inaccurate.[3] Sergio was not throwing rocks; he was hiding, making the fatal mistake of peeking to see if the agent was still present. In spite of the cell phone videos, the Department of Justice ruled that insufficient evidence existed to prosecute Mesa on any criminal or civil charges. Since 2010 (until March 2015) border agents have killed thirty-three individuals, at least twelve of them American citizens. Besides José and Sergio, others where shot from the U.S. side of the wall while they were in Mexico: Ramses Barron Torres (age seventeen) who was accused of throwing rocks, although denied by witnesses; Carlos Lamadrid (age nineteen) a U.S. citizen shot three times in the back for throwing rocks after fleeing into Mexico; Jose Alfredo Yañez Reyes (age forty) killed as he prepared to cross the border, accused of throwing rocks; Juan Pablo Perez Santillán (age thirty), killed while standing on the banks of the Rio Grande, accused of throwing rocks, although witnesses claim he was unarmed; and Guillermo Arévalo Pedroza (age thirty-six), who was not trying to enter the U.S., but nonetheless was killed in front of his wife and small daughters while barbecuing, allegedly he was throwing rocks even though a video of the shooting fails to show any rock being thrown.[4]

"Rocking" usually occurs for the purpose of distracting agents from apprehending drug mules or immigrants trying to make it across the wall. According to a March 7, 2014 memo to all personnel written by Michael J. Fisher, Chief U.S. Border Patrol, agents have been assaulted with rocks

3. https://www.youtube.com/watch?v=7wI2Q1XikLw.
4. https://www.youtube.com/watch?v=b1vu1qvm7QM.

1,713 times since 2010 (although how these numbers were arrived at, remains a mystery). In these situations, agents responded forty-three times with deadly force resulting in the death of ten individuals.[5] Most agents respond to rock throwers with a long-range FN-303 rifle style weapon that shoots ten pepper spray balls a second, designed to saturate an area with irritating vapors causing rock throwers to simply disperse. While it is true that twenty-two Border agents have died in the line of duty since 2004, all, with the exception of four, died in vehicle or training accidents. Of the four who died in direct conflict with an aggressor, one agent, Nicholas Ivie, died due to "friendly fire" at the hands of another agent eight days and about seventy miles west from where José died. Even though the memo goes on to state that Border agents are at greater risk than other law enforcement agencies; the reality is that it is much safer being a Border Patrol agent than an Arizona police officer who is five times more likely to face an assault and four times more likely to be assaulted with a deadly weapon.

Killing Mexicans on their own soil occurs with minor public repercussions. With the exception of administrative leave, in none of the multiple uses of deadly force by the Border Patrol, even when they killed Americans, did an agent face any consequences from the Justice Department, Homeland Security, or the Customs and Border Protection.[6] Border Patrol may announce the start of an investigation, but soon afterwards, the investigation is sealed from public scrutiny. Years pass before some announcement is quietly made that the agent was cleared of any wrongdoings and the case is closed. On September 23, 2015, the case of José Antonio Elena Rodríguez, unlike so many others, led to an indictment of officer Lonnie Swartz by a federal grand

5. Fisher, "Use of Safe Tactics."
6. Ortega and O'Dell, "Deadly Border Agent Incidents."

jury on the charge of second-degree murder. For the first time in U.S. history, a Border Patrol agent was arraigned for killing a Mexican national across the international border. Conviction, nonetheless, may prove difficult due to the benefit of the doubt usually given to border agents, not to mention the sympathy they usually receive by the government for supposedly "placing their lives on the line." When two agents, Ignacio Ramos and Jose Compean, were convicted for shooting an unarmed drug trafficker who was running away, they had their sentences commuted by President George W. Bush on his last day in office. We are left to wonder what would happen if Mexican authorities were habitually shooting into the U.S. and killing unarmed Anglo teenage boys? How differently would such cases be treated? Different responses simply unmask differing values placed upon white lives as oppose to brown lives, stressing that the former matters more than the latter.

Blaming a handful of rogue officers cannot dismiss the killing of Mexican teenagers on their own soil by Border Patrol agents. These killings are symptomatic of institutional dysfunction. This was made clear by a report commissioned by U.S. Customs and Border Protection and conducted by the Police Executive Research Forum (a nonprofit group that advices law enforcement agencies) after Border Patrol was pressured to conduct such a review by sixteen members of Congress on May 2010. The report examined all events that included deadly force from January 2010 through October 2012. According to the report, border agents would deliberately step in the paths of vehicles to justify shooting the drivers, and shoot rock throwers out of frustration rather than any life-threatening concerns. More damning, the report found that the agency lacked diligence in investigating the firing of weapons by agents.[7] In spite of the incriminatory report, an internal response marked "Law Enforcement Sensitive," rejected the recommendations barring border agents from shooting at vehicles or rock throwers if their lives are not in danger.[8] And even though no border agent has ever lost her or his life as a result of a thrown rock, Border Patrol Chief Fisher, in a memo written to all personnel after the release of the Police Executive Research Forum's report, continues to consider rocks to be a deadly weapon that justifies lethal force.[9]

Gloria E. Anzaldúa best captures what this border truly signifies.

> The U.S-Mexican border *es una herida abierta* [an open wound] where the Third World grates against the first and bleeds. And before a scab forms it hemorrhages again, the lifeblood of two worlds merging to form a third country—a border culture. Borders are set up to define the places that are safe and unsafe, to distinguish us from them. A border is a dividing line, a narrow strip along a steep edge. A borderland is a vague and undetermined place created by the emotional residue of an unnatural boundary. It is in a constant state of transition. The prohibited and forbidden are its inhabitants.[10]

As I look at the wall across the street from where José brutally died, I notice that upon the steel posts someone stenciled white candles and yellow doves, so as not to forget José Antonio Elena Rodríguez. A few feet away from where José laid bleeding, on the concrete embark that leads up to

7. Police Executive Research Forum, *Use of Force Review*, 4, 6–7.

8. Bennett, "Border Patrol's Use of Deadly Force."

9. Fisher, "Use of Safe Tactics."

10. Anzaldúa, *Borderlands/La Frontera*, 3.

the wall, someone spray-painted the words, "*CHINGA LA MIGRA.*"

This artificial line that we call a border stretches from San Diego, California to Brownsville, Texas, and represents the most frequently crossed international border in the world. The U.S. and Mexico are not in a state of war; nevertheless, this border is among the most militarized in the world contributing to war-zone mentality. The entire southern border is not fenced; only about 670 miles have a physical wall.[11] When building the wall, then Department of Homeland Security Secretary, Michael Chertoff, waived thirty-six federal and state environmental laws in order to quickly complete construction, disrupting animal migration patterns and causing degradation along fragile ecological wildlife refuges.[12]

The Border Patrol spent $2.4 billion to build these 670 miles of fence from 2006 to 2009, or about $3 million a mile (these numbers do not include the lifetime maintenance cost of about $50 billion). Natural barriers such as the rapid flowing Rio Grande (although word "grande"—big—is a misnomer as some parts of the river are narrow and shallow) or the scorching Sonora Desert demarcate the parts of the border where the wall is absent. Still, Congress continues to debate adding an addition 700 miles of fencing. All paved roads entering the U.S. from Mexico are blocked and heavily patrolled. But along a thin line in the sand, at times noticeable by only a three-wire barbed cattle fence that runs through hazardous remote mountains and wilderness, crossing is risky but possible. From 2001 to 2013, $186 billion was spent on border security; $18 billion in 2013 alone.[13]

11. Sheldon, "Operation Streamline," 92.
12. Archibold, "Government Issues Waiver."
13. "NAFTA at 20."

Border security falls under the jurisdiction of Customs and Border Protection, a component of the Department of Homeland Security. About twelve million individuals evenly live along both sides of this artificial line. The Secure Fence Act of 2006 constructed the wall to cover about one third of the border, replacing the earlier solid wall. Regardless of the type of fence built, it will not accomplish its task of keeping out those whom the U.S. define as undesirable. When Department of Homeland Security Secretary Janet Napolitano served as Governor of Arizona, she quipped, "You show me a fifty foot wall and I'll show you a fifty-one foot ladder at the border."

Forgotten in our current immigration discourse is that not long ago (1942–64), documented Mexican immigration flourished. Under the Bracero Program, more than four million Mexicans worked on U.S. farms. By the late 1950s, during the height of the program, an average of 438,000 workers crossed the borders with proper documentation. These brown hands built a formidable U.S. agricultural center. For a multitude of reasons, including abuses of farm workers, documented immigration came to an end; nonetheless, farm workers continued to enter the country during the harvest to continue picking American crops, only now without proper documentation. Between 1965 and 1985, millions of undocumented workers crossed the border for work and returned home after the harvest.

When migration was more fluid, the import of seasonal workers was beneficial for both countries and encouraged. Farmers would advertise for workers in Mexican border town newspapers in Spanish, directing prospective laborers to the appropriate church parking lot for a ride to the fields. The migrant journey would begin by simply crossing over at urban border cities or towns. The migrant would make his (seldom her) way as far north as possible, and then follow the harvest seasons southwards. Eventually, they would return to their own lands and family in Mexico, relying on the extra funds earned in *el Norte* to make improvements to their homes and farms, advance their family's meager fortunes, and contribute to their communities. Migration was based on an eight to nine-month cycle of working north of the border followed by months at home to attend to their own October harvest and the year-end religious holidays.

Even though millions crossed the border, only about 150,000 per year actually stayed and settled in the United States with an additional 59,000 arriving to stay with proper documentation.[14] This "wink and a nod" law enforcement allowed U.S. farmers to get their crops harvested and offered Mexican workers the ability to provide for their families back home. The real job of the Border Patrol was to make sure these workers returned at the conclusion of the harvest. What was once a circular migration became permanent with the erection of the fence. The border wall has had two immediate results. First, fewer field hands created chaos in the agricultural industry. In 2006, twenty percent of agricultural products were not picked. The 2007 figures were estimated to reach thirty percent. Michigan growers were forced to leave their asparagus in the fields to rot, while North Carolina farmers lost nearly a third of their cucumber crop.[15] And second, those coming to work on farms were forced to pay higher costs, in monetary and human terms, to the coyotes—whose power is strengthened and solidified—due to the need of being led through mountainous terrain and treacherous deserts.

Since those simpler days, the border has become a militarized zone where constitutional guarantees and

14. Massey, "Foreword," in *Latinas/os in the United States*, xi.
15. "Immigration Non-Harvest."

international laws are routinely ignored. Our efforts to secure the southern border results in the institutionalization of human and civil rights violations evident by increasing migrant deaths, along with a corrupting influence upon under-trained law enforcement officers. The danger of a militarized border can be illustrated by the June 12, 1992 shooting of twenty-six-year-old Dario Miranda Valenzuela who was unarmed—just one example of many. While crossing the border through a well-lit canyon that clearly indicated Valenzuela was unarmed, he was shot twice in the back by Border Patrol Agent Michael Elmer with a high-powered AR-15 rifle from a distance of 150 feet. Eduardo Torres Berber, Valenzuela's brother-in-law who was with him that fateful early evening, fled back to Mexico; but he recalled there were no warning shots. Once Valenzuela was shot, he looked up to see Elmer yelling at him in Spanish "I am going to kill you." As a wounded Valenzuela bled, officer Elmer dragged Valenzuela fifty yards in an attempt to hide the body, planning to return the next day and cover up the incident by burying him. Tragically, if Valenzuela was to be given proper medical aid, he could have survived his wounds; instead, he was left to slowly bleed to death, a process that took about thirty minutes. When the incident was uncovered, Elmer became the first border agent ever brought to trial, but was acquitted by a jury who concluded he acted in self-defense from a "drug smuggler" in a tense "war zone." Ironically, Elmer was previously investigated by the Justice Department for stealing cocaine from a major drug bust and selling the stolen substance.[16]

This artificial line, and its consequences in terms of the carnage of brown bodies, is a product of empire building.

16. Rotella, "Ex-Border Patrol Agent Acquitted"; McDonnell, "Official Says Border Killing Victim"; McDonnell, "Border Patrol Agent Charged.

For the United States to exist, the indigenous population had to either be evicted or exterminated. The body count of native people due to exposure of European diseases such as smallpox was understood as divine providence. John Winthrop, a leading figure in the founding of the Massachusetts Bay Colony and creator of the "city upon a hill" mythology, saw the decimation of Indians by European diseases as God "making room" for Euroamericans by "clear[ing their] title to this place."[17] As the young Republic moved westward, divine inspiration under the guise of the romanticized jingoism known as Manifest Destiny justified land thief. John O'Sullivan, editor of the *Democratic Review*, captured this pseudo-religious sentiment when he wrote: "Our manifest destiny to overspread the continent allotted by Providence for the free development of our yearly multiplying millions."[18]

Just as the Almighty gave Israel of old a Promised Land; so too does the God of the new Republic bestow upon Euroamericans, due to their racial superiority, a "virgin land" with a mandate to "tame the wilderness" and take possession of the entire continent. And just as the Hebrew God called for the genocide of all who stood in their way (Exod 23:23), so too would the God of this New Israel—God's new chosen people—demand violently taking possession of the land occupied by their Canaanites going under names like Osage, Cherokee, or Arapahoe. This New Jerusalem was called to fulfill its manifest destiny by spreading its Protestant Gospel wings across an entire hemisphere, from the Arctic north to the Isthmus south, in the hopes of converting the savagery of "primitive tribes" and the "heresy" of Roman Catholicism in the southwest. Manifest Destiny

17. Takaki, *A Different Mirror,* 39–40.
18. O'Sullivan, "Annexation," 5.

was a post-millennialist[19] religious ideology that believed God's celestial Kingdom would be realized after the U.S. accomplished its apocalyptic mission of occupying the new "Promised Land," ushering Christ's second coming.[20]

This religious ideology took on political ramifications as Anglo-Saxons attempted to fulfill their providential mission of expanding white civilization and institutions across North America. Missouri Senator Thomas Hart Benton (1821–51) articulates this divine mission, seeing the "white" race following the "divine command to subdue and replenish the earth," by destroying "savagery," and replacing the "wigwam" by the "Capitol," the "savage" with the "Christian," and the "red squaws" with the "white matrons."[21] Not only must the Western Hemisphere bend its knees before the ideology of Manifest Destiny, but so too must the entire world. In 1885, influential minister and leader of the Social Gospel Movement, Josiah Strong, saw the white race as being responsible for extending Christianity throughout the world. He wrote:

> It seems to me that God, with infinite wisdom and skill, is training the Anglo-Saxon race for an hour sure to come in the world's future. . . . If I read not amiss, this powerful race will move down upon Mexico, down upon Central and South America, out upon the islands of the sea, over upon Africa and beyond. And can any one doubt that the result of this competition of races will be the "survival of the fittest"?[22]

19. Post-millennialism was a prevalent theological concept that dealt with the second-coming of Christ, a return that would occur after a thousand years (hence post-millennial) of God's Kingdom being established on earth.

20. Ahlstrom, *A Religious History*, 845, 877–78.

21. Takaki, *A Different Mirror*, 191.

22. Smith, *What Happened in Cuba?*, 85–87.

The ideology of Manifest Destiny initiated the conquest of Texas and northern Mexico and extended U.S. boundaries, physically possessing and repopulating the new lands. Perhaps the staunchest supporter of Manifest Destiny was James K. Polk, eleventh president, who while on the campaign trail promised to annex Texas and engage Mexico in war if elected. Once taking office, he deployed troops into Mexican territory to solicit the desired response of having the Mexican army first fire upon the invading U.S. army. Polk then requested a declaration of war from Congress. The Mexican-American War ended with Mexico's capitulation and the signing of the 1848 Treaty of Guadalupe-Hidalgo, which ceded half of her territory to the United States. A surveyor line was drawn across the sand upon an area that, according to the archeological evidence, has historically experienced fluid migration.

Acquiring land had more to do then simply divine inspiration. With the new possessions came all the gold deposits in California, copper deposits in Arizona and New Mexico, silver deposits in Nevada, oil in Texas, and all of the natural harbors (except Veracruz) necessary for commerce along the California coast. By ignoring the provisions of the peace treaty signed with Mexico, the U.S. government was able to dismiss the historic land titles Mexicans held, allowing white U.S. citizens to obtain the natural resources embedded in the land. These natural resources, along with cheap Mexican labor allowed the overall U.S. economy to develop and function, while economically dooming Mexico by preventing the nation from capitalizing on its stolen natural resources.

As I stand beside the fence, looking into the United States, I become unmistakably aware that this monstrous wall is a consequence of U.S. conquest, of a nineteenth-century land grab where a powerful nation created a religious justification to disrespect the sovereignty of another nation. As Mexicans walk by me going about their daily errands, and as I look back to see the face of José Antonio Elena Rodríguez staring back at me from a handbill posted on the clinic wall were he perished, I can't help but notice that they are all mostly *indios*, a mestizaje of the original indigenous people of the land and their Spaniard colonizers. As I think of the Indian blood that flows through their veins, I am reminded that their ancestors once freely crossed a land now scarred by a wall erected by a European concept of nation-state demarcated through the use of firearms.

That afternoon, a few blocks from the international fence, I meet Maria as she prepares to cross the line to find work in the U.S. This is not the first time she attempts a crossing. Maria is wearing several layers of clothes even though it is a warm day. All of her possessions are in a grocery plastic bag. She is, not surprisingly, anxious about the hazards of crossing. Coyotes, those who smuggle people across the border, have been known to coerce, rape, and force migrants into sexual servitude until their debts are paid.[23] The possibility of being raped is so high that many women and girls inject contraceptives before attempting a crossing.[24] Maria must also avoid what she calls "migrant hunters," white supremacist vigilante groups such as the American Patrol or the Minutemen, that harass migrants. Some migrants have reported being "shot at, bitten by dogs, hit with flashlights, kicked, taunted, and unlawfully imprisoned" by these vigilante groups.[25]

Maria must be in her late thirties, about five feet tall, with pronounced indigenous features. I stoop down

---

23. Ogren, "Migration and Human Rights," 226.

24. Ibid., 221–22.

25. American Civil Liberties Union, *Creating the Minutemen*, 13.

to speak to her, asking what she would like Americans to know. She thinks for just a few seconds before responding:

> They too were immigrants. I don't believe that the United States citizen was born an American; because what I know is that the Mayans are the legitimate Americans. Not the American citizen, I want them to show respect. And just like their forefathers were respected, that they should learn to respect us who are Mexicans.

As I ponder Maria's comments, I cannot help but be reminded of the often-quoted retort from late Mexican president Porfirio Diaz (1873–1911), "Poor Mexico, so far from God, so close to the United States."

DISCUSSION QUESTIONS

- If soldiers or law enforcement officers in Mexico were to shoot over the international border and kill a U.S. teenage citizen, should the shooter be held liable in U.S. courts? What penalties and responsibilities would Mexico have toward the family of the murdered child or to the U.S. government? How should the soldier or law enforcement officer be held accountable? Should Mexico fully cooperate with the investigation? Should the U.S. be held to a similar standard if one of its soldiers or law enforcement officers kills a Mexican citizen? Why or why not?

- Gloria E. Anzaldúa describes the U.S.-Mexican border as *una herida abierta*. What does she mean by this? Is her description accurate? Why or why not? What have been the consequences of militarizing the southern international border? What has been the impact to communities along the border? To U.S. citizens? To

Mexican citizens?

- Describe the religious and political ideologies under-girding our current immigration policies. How long did it take to create the current crises on our southern borders? Why are those immigrants coming from Mexico (and Central America) different from other groups migrating to the U.S.? What historical considerations should be kept in mind when exploring these differences?

2

DOWNTOWN CRAWFORDSVILLE, INDIANA

WHAT DOES A SMALL Midwestern town located somewhere in Indiana have to do with Mexican immigration? One can never truly understand our current immigration crisis unless they pay close attention to Crawfordsville, a small community of about 16,000 mainly white inhabitants located in the American heartland, about an hour's drive northwest of Indianapolis. A colleague who lives in town reminds me, "if you go a mile in any direction, you will hit cornfields." It is the presence of these cornfields that is partially responsible for our current immigration crisis.

The town, started in 1813, is named in honor of Colonel William H. Crawford who fought in the French and Indian War and the American Revolutionary War. He was a surveyor for and friend of George Washington, burned at the stake by indigenous people (the Lenape) in retaliation for the Gnadenhutten massacre that took place during the closing days of the American Revolution. Nicknamed the Athens of Indiana, Crawfordsville serves as the county seat for Montgomery County. In 1832, Wabash College, an all-male liberal arts school, made its home in Crawfordsville and continues to attract young men to the area. Andrew Carnegie chose the town to build his first Indiana library in 1902, either an attempt to rehabilitate his image after, or penitence for, his bloody response to the 1892 Homestead Strike. Crawfordsville is probably best known for the house located at 200 Wallace Avenue, the former home of Lew Wallace, Civil War Major General, diplomat, inventor, and author of *Ben-Hur*.

According to the 2010 census, about 1,300 Latinxs (or 8.2 percent of the population) live in the city.[1] With the exception of the three local Mexican Restaurants, it would seem that this small community in the Midwest has few if any ties with the Latinx community. Nevertheless, as I sit on a hot summer day on the steps of the Montgomery County Courthouse, located on East Main Street, I remain cognizant that the space I am currently occupying is directly connected with the oppression I witnessed on the U.S.-Mexican border a few months earlier. We may be 1,400 miles from the border; nevertheless, the reason for the wall separating the two countries is linked to this small community and hundreds of other communities like this one that make up the Corn Belt.

Corn, better known as maize, is the miracle crop, which flourishes in areas below sea levels and at altitudes as high as 12,000 feet; in dry areas that receive twelve inches of rainfall per year and in humid areas with 400 inches of yearly rainfall. First cultivated some 5,600 to 7,000 years ago

---

1. http://factfinder.census.gov/faces/tableservices/jsf/pages/productview.xhtml?src=CF.

in the Tehuacán Valley (known as the "Cradle of Corn"), the crop spread throughout Mesoamerica. The first fossils of maize pollen, dating over 80,000 years ago, have been discovered in lake sediment beneath Mexico City. Maize is foundational to the ancient Mayan and Aztec cosmologies, evident in the fact that Mayans, who believe humans were created from maize, refer to themselves as the people of the corn. Maize transformed the Mesoamerica region into a major pre-capitalist commodity production and exchange center. Along with beans and squash, the three crops—referred to by native people as the "three sisters"—have for millenniums been the main food source. But maize is more than the traditional staple of the Mexican diet; the husks are dried and used, as in the case of wrapping tamales, the cobs are burned as fuel, the leftover stalks is used as animal feed, and various parts of the maize plant decorate homes during religious festivals. From Mesoamerica, the crop made its way south and north, introduced to northern indigenous nations by way of the Chihuahuan and Sonoran deserts, whose ancient trails are currently blocked by the international wall. Eventually a lost Columbus, discovered by the indigenous people, brought the crop to Europe where it spread.

Maize comes from a plant that does not exist naturally in the wild, but requires human cultivation. The indigenous people treated this crop as sacred, serving as an offering to Aztec deities as illustrated on ancient rock paintings. Respect for maize continues to this day, illustrated when Mexican farmers chant and pray for a successful crop as they sprinkle cornmeal on their fields facing the four directions. For centuries, Mexican farmers cultivated maize in the same way as their ancestors, reserving a third of the crop to feed the family, and the rest to be sold at local markets. All this changed with the ratification of the North

American Free Trade Agreement (NAFTA), a neoliberal U.S. trade agreement with Canada and Mexico, the first and third largest trading partner respectively.

Hardest hit by the effects of NAFTA were the rural *campesinos* ("peasants"). As owners or renters of land, they were conceptualized as minor producers whose unpaid labor mainly provided for their own consumption, and at times, for exchange or sale in the marketplace. The Mexican government regarded these *campesinos* as failing to maximize agricultural returns; thus the government moved to dismantle what they saw as a backward, unprofitable, stubborn, indigenous tradition. Through NAFTA, a concerted shift was made from national food self-sufficiency to reliance on food imports. In the eyes of the Mexican government, neither indigenous communities nor *campesinos* were needed to build a nation interconnected to the global neoliberal economic order; instead, what was needed was the movement of surplus labor to manufacturing plants known as *maquiladoras* (or *maquilas*).[2]

President Bill Clinton signed the trilateral free-trade deal known as NAFTA, a brainchild of Ronald Reagan, into existence on January 1994. NAFTA was designed to freely move goods across borders, free from tariffs or taxes to be fully faded out by 2008. Economists point out that NAFTA simply accelerated the trade liberalization that was already occurring, concluding that the changes brought about by the agreement would have eventually taken place with or without the agreement.[3] Nevertheless, when the agreement was signed into law, there was an expectation that a financial bonanza would develop for U.S. exporters, and high-paying jobs would be created for U.S. workers. NAFTA was supposed to also benefit the Mexican workers by moving them

2. Fitting, *Struggle for Maize*, 21–22, 103, 109.

3. Villarreal and Fergusson, "North American Free Trade," ii.

from the drain on scarce government resources incurred in smallholder maize production toward modernization and globalization ushered in by free markets, thus reducing income disparities between Mexico and its two northern neighbors. In reality, by the second year of the implementation of NAFTA, the price of grain dropped by 48 percent, a saving not passed on to the Mexican consumer. By 2006, corn based tortillas rose about 738 percent in price.[4]

Originally, a fifteen-year period for gradually raising the amount of U.S. corn that could enter Mexico without tariffs was part of the NAFTA agreement. But in less than three years, Mexico unilaterally lifted the corn quotas to assist its chicken and pork industries. Mexican NAFTA negotiators suspended quotas to directly benefit fellow negotiator Eduardo Bours, whose family owns the largest chicken farm in Mexico. Lifting quotas financially rewarded his family business, although Mexico lost some $2 billion in tariffs as about half a million maize farmers abandoned their lands and moved to the cities in hope of finding a new livelihood.[5] By 2000, Mexico experienced one million lost jobs due to NAFTA.[6]

By January 1, 2008, Mexico repealed all tariffs on corn imported from the north leading to massive protest. Within a month, hundreds of thousands of farmers were clogging the streets of central Mexico City protesting the entry of cheap imported corn from the United States and Canada. According to Ramon Garcia, a maize *campesino* just outside Mexico City, he could no longer afford to fertilize his crop or rent a tractor to till his field. The work is too much for such low returns. "Corn is too cheap," according to Garcia,

4. Fitting, *Struggle for Maize*, 202–4.

5. Rosenberg, "Free-Trade Fix," and "Why Mexico's Small Corn Farmers Go Hungry."

6. Scott, et al., "Revisiting NAFTA," 43.

"for me to make a profit, it has to bring in 15 pesos ($1.4) a kilo, and I can barely get 10."[7] Another maize *campesino* from the Yucatán, Enrique Barrera Pérez, expressed his frustration, stating, "We cannot compete against this monster, the United States. It's not worth the trouble to plant. We don't have the subsidies. We don't have the machinery."[8] Contrary to NAFTA promises, Mexican per capita income during the first two decades of NAFTA rose a mere 1.2 percent and nearly doubled the number of Mexican-born people living in the U.S.[9]

Sin maíz, no hay país. Maize best signifies how NAFTA advanced the neoliberal threat and chaos visited upon *campesinos*, and by extension, Mexican sovereignty and culture. The land where maize was first domesticated has been transformed into the land dependent on U.S. corn imports. Studying the impact of NAFTA, the Carnegie Endowment for International Peace concluded that ten years of NAFTA has brought hardship to hundreds of thousands of subsistence farmers.[10] Francisco Javier Réos, a fifteen-acres maize *campesino* from Bahia de Banderas in the State of Nayarit used to depend on a $3,000 to $4,000 profit margin. But with the 2008 final lifting of the last tariffs on U.S. corn (as well as beans, sugar, and milk), Mr. Réos worries he will not be able to stay in business. According to Mexican officials, four-fifths of the nation's 2.6 million small farms have such small plots that they produce just enough to live on, creating a northward migration push.[11]

So what does the plight of Mexican maize farmers have to do with Crawfordsville corn farmers, and farmers

7. Whitneck, "Mexican Farmers Protest NAFTA."

8. McKinley, Jr. "Mexican Farmers Protest."

9. Sergie, "NAFTA's Economic Impact," 4.

10. Bello, "World Bank"; Dugger, "Report Finds Few Benefits."

11. McKinley, "Mexican Farmers Protest."

throughout the U.S. Corn Belt? Because the United States subsidizes U.S. farmers, by underwriting the cost of their crops (especially corn), U.S. farmers are able to sell their crops below international market price. According to the Environmental Working Group, of the $277.3 billion spent between 1995 (second year of NAFTA) through 2011 in subsidies to U.S. farmers, a total over $81.7 billion went specifically to corn producers.[12] James D. Wolfensohn, who served as the president of the World Bank from 1995 to 2005, claims farm subsidies from wealthy nations at a tune of about $1 billion a day is devastating impoverished countries. Reducing these subsidies, he says, is the most important act industrial nations can implement to eradicate poverty among millions of the world's poor.[13]

When we recall the first presidential caucus is held in Iowa, the buckle of the Corn Belt, we should not be surprised that the political will to eradicate the global injustice of U.S. corn subsidies will fail to be raised. Dumping U.S. surplus of subsidized corn (at about $4 billion a year from 1995 to 2004)[14] on Mexico meant a 70 percent drop in Mexican maize prices, while housing, food, and other living essentials increased by 247 percent.[15] In the first decade of NAFTA, at least 1.3 million Mexican maize *campesinos* lost their small plots of land, unable to compete with cheaper U.S. subsidized corn.[16] With the Mexican farmer squeezed out due to their inability to compete with U.S. subsidized

12. http://farm.ewg.org/region.php?fips=00000&regname=UnitedStatesFarmSubsidySummary.

13. Andrews, "Rich Nations Criticized,"; Becker, "Western Farmers."

14. Barrionuevo, "Mountains of Corn."

15 López, *Farmworkers' Journal*, 7–9, 41.

16. Labor Council for Latin American Advancement (LCLAA), *Another America Is Possible*, 4–8.

corn, U.S.-owned transnational traders, like Cargill and Maseca, were able to step in and monopolize the corn sector by speculating on trading trends. They used their power within the market to manipulate movements on biofuel demand and thus artificially inflate the price of corn many times over.[17] Worsening the plight of the maize *campesino* were the structural adjustments imposed on Mexico by the World Bank in 1991, which eliminated all government price supports and subsidies for Mexican corn.[18]

Big Corn is king, ruling over a quarter of all U.S. agricultural acreage under cultivation. The average person in the U.S. consumes about one ton of corn a year, mostly in the form of high-fructose corn syrup in soft drinks and processed foods, and in the form of chicken and meat that ingests corn as animal feed. The U.S., thanks to government subsidies, has become the largest producer and exporter of corn in the world.[19] Because agriculture is one of the few sectors of the economy where the United States runs a trade surplus, there is no hurry to change this global economic relationship. Complicating the demand for corn is the huge corn ethanol mandate by Congress that burns food in the failed attempt to produce motor fuel. A multibillion-dollar network of over two hundred distilleries is created, tasked with producing gasoline, even though no motor fuel shortage exists. What does exist is a growing global shortage of food.[20]

This Congressional mandate has lead to higher food prices, increased air and water pollution, and greater water consumption. Ironically, if all the corn grown in the U.S. were turned into ethanol, it would barely meet six

17. Bello, "World Bank."
18. De La Torre, *Trails of Hope and Terror*, 39.
19. Fitting, *Struggle for Maize*, 46–47.
20. Bryce, "Ethanol Scam," 91–93.

percent of the U.S. fuel needs. The billions of corn bushels relegated to ethanol production is twice as much as all the corn produced by the entire European Union and five times as much as Mexico.[21] Ethanol production, according to a 2008 World Bank report, was a major contributor to the declining global price of corn that devastated the Mexican *campesino*. According to the report: "Without the increase in biofuels, global wheat and maize stocks would not have declined appreciably and price increases due to other factors would have been moderate."[22]

Corn is not the only commodity that links the good folks of Crawfordsville with Mexico. If I walk a block north on N. Washington Avenue (State Road 231) I discover a Walgreens and a CVS catty-corner from each other. I enter the stores to browse. Walking the isles of Walgreens I notice they are selling bottles of Broncolin Honey Syrup dietary supplement and X-L 3 Cold Medicine tablets. I cross the street to CVS and find Vicks VaboRub and Clairol Hair Coloring. These four items are but a few of the numerous products sold by these two competing businesses that were once made in the U.S., employing American workers, but are now made in Mexico, thanks mainly to NAFTA.

U.S. owned maquiladoras along the southern side of the U.S. Mexican border import and assemble duty-free components for export. These plants allow its U.S. owners (as well as some Mexican and Asian owners) to profit from low wages and by the duty that is charged only on the "value added"—understood as the value of the finished product minus the total cost of the imported components. In effect, Mexican labor is exported disembodied from the flesh and blood Mexican to whom said labor is attached. The border fence that attempts to be impenetrable when it comes to the

21. Ibid.

22. Mitchell, "Note on Rising Food Prices," 16.

movement of human bodies remains porous to neoliberalism as U.S. corn flows southwards and cheap labor from maquiladoras flows northward unabated.

These maquiladoras have become a refuge to former Mexican *campesinos*, who once lived off maize farming, but now realize that they can no longer compete with agricultural subsidized goods imported from the United States. With few options for financial self-sufficiency, they move northward to the industrial areas along the border to find employment. Most move to *las colonias* (poor, sprawling slums of shacks patched together from pieces of metal, wood, and plastic) that surround the maquilas. Every rural peasant forced to leave the land means another producer is forced to migrate to the city and, along with their family, become consumers. This migration contributes to the perpetual need for future food aid. Thanks to NAFTA, they were forced to immigrate to large Mexican cities where high unemployment rates keep wages depressed.

Opening these maquiladoras has also negatively impacted American workers, forcing them to compete in the neoliberal global labor market against Mexicans paid a fraction for the same work. Take for example the Maytag refrigerator plant that was located in the prairie town of Galesburg, Illinois, about a three-and-a-half-hour drive northwest of Crawfordsville. The plant once employed 1,600 workers of Galesburg's 34,000 residents. On October 2002, Maytag announced that by 2004, it was moving its profitable Galesburg plant to Reynosa, Mexico. At the time, Maytag was paying an average of $15.14 an hour to its Galesburg employees. But by moving the plant to Reynosa, Maytag could pay an average of $2.00 an hour. The day the plant closure was announced, Maytag's stocks jumped 6 percent to the applause of Wall Street. Besides the direct loss of sixteen hundred jobs, an additional two thousand jobs that depended on the plant (in distribution and auxiliary industries) were phased out. Home prices took a downward turn and an oversaturated pool of unemployed workers depressed regional wages.[23] What Galesburg faced is but an example of what has continuously occurred throughout U.S. towns and cities since NAFTA: corporate managers force workers to accept lower wages and benefits, threatening that if they don't, their jobs will be exported to Mexico. Even after the workers agreed to salary cuts, jobs went south anyway.

U.S. corporate quest for the lowest possible wage has been the main reason industries relocated south of the border. During the first ten years since NAFTA was implemented, some 780,000 jobs in textile and apparel manufacturing were lost.[24] That "great sucking sound" (to quote Ross Perot) we heard was U.S. jobs going to Mexico. Prior to the start of NAFTA (1993), the U.S. maintained a $1.7 billion trade surplus with Mexico; five years after NAFTA, the surplus plunged to a $12.5 billion deficit, reaching a $53.8 billion deficit by 2014. According to the Economic Policy Institute calculations, an estimated 1.5 million jobs were eliminated from the U.S. by 2011 due to Mexican imports.[25] A race to the lowest possible wage has outsourced U.S. production, which in turn further destroyed the U.S. industrial base by reducing manufacturing jobs, shifting the focus to lower paying service jobs.

Yet, it would be erroneous to assume that Mexicans experienced a windfall. While American workers suffered under NAFTA, Mexicans sank into deeper poverty. In 1975, Mexican production workers earned 23 percent of

23. Greenhouse, "City Feels Early Effects."

24. LCLAA and Public Citizen, *Another America Is Possible*, 5.

25. Barlett and Steele, *Betrayal of the American Dream*, 55–56; Villarreal and Fergusson, "North American Free Trade," 14.

U.S. wages. Since the relocation of U.S. jobs to Mexico, that number dropped to 11 percent. Women fared worse, with a poverty rate for households headed by a woman increasing by 50 percent.[26] By 2014, the federal minimum wage was 67 Mexican pesos a day, or about $5.12 in U.S. dollars. Since 1976, the last time the federal minimum wage was raised, Mexican wages lost 71 percent of its purchasing value.[27] Mexican 2014 poverty rate (defined as living on 2,542 pesos a month or $157.70 in U.S. dollars) stands at 46.2 percent, or about 55.3 of the 120 million inhabitants.[28]

Exacerbating Mexican poverty are abuses occurring in maquiladoras. Despite the expanding trade rhetoric used to justify NAFTA (after all, trade between the U.S., Mexico, and Canada was expanding), its main purpose was to free U.S. corporations from U.S. laws designed to protect workers and the environment from abuses; hence, no provisions were written into the agreement, although side pacts were negotiated afterwards. Still, free from U.S. child labor laws, children as young as nine work in the maquilas. These children abandon their studies for the illusion of freedom that comes with wages. Because they usually provide half their earnings to the parents, contributing to the survival of the family, a silence is created concerning the continuation of the children's education on the part of the parents.[29] Free from U.S. environmental laws, runoff wastewater from the maquila threatens an already overburdened water and agricultural system.[30] Poor government oversight has led to the improper disposal of hazardous waste products leading to the gradual deterioration of the urban communities where

26. LCLAA and Public Citizen, *Another America Is Possible*, 5.

27. Montes, "Mexico Looks to Raise Wages."

28. Reuters, "Mexico Poverty Rate."

29. Fitting, *Struggle for Maize*, 177, 213.

30. Ibid., 178.

the maquilas are located.[31] Free from U.S. workplace safety regulations, few, if any recourses exist for those injured on the job.

The U.S. public scapegoats the Mexican migrant for the current immigration crisis, even though NAFTA is the main reason why undocumented migrants reside in the U.S., a consequence of what immigration experts call the "push-and-pull" factor. The economic condition existing in the immigrant's homeland, due in part to our corn subsidies, "pushes" them out, while the U.S. need for cheap labor "pulls" them in. The undocumented presence in the U.S. is not their attempt to force themselves upon an unwilling host country; rather it is the result of economic conditions created, in good measure, by U.S. trade and foreign policies. One of the reasons we have an immigration crisis is because our trade policies are geared, thanks to subsidized corn (as well as other agricultural goods), to profit U.S. businesses at the expense of farmers in two-third world nations. When a *campesino* is no longer able to grow his or her crops because of the inability to compete in the marketplace with U.S. subsidized produce, they have little choice but to abandon their lands—that is the land of their ancestors—and venture into the cities with the hope of finding jobs in one of the maquiladoras.

Even if they obtain employment at a maquila, wages earned fall short of their hope to survive financially. Unfortunately, a lack of a living wage is but one of the negative impacts NAFTA has had on Mexicans who, with the exception of Haiti, have the lowest minimum wage in the hemisphere. For the former maize *campesino*, now working in one of the maquiladoras for a few dollars a day, all they need to do is look across the border fence and see through the gaps the McDonald's on the other side, where a pimple-faced high

31. Godoy, "Mexico: Maquiladora Factories."

school kid can make more in a few hours than the former farmer can make in a week. If only the former *campesinos* could cross the border, then they could again feed their families. No doubt, the *campesinos* would probably have been happier providing for the families the way their ancestors have done for centuries. But NAFTA has changed the equation for the poor. Working on someone else's land in a different nation becomes the new hope for survival.

I walk back toward Main Street and hang a left, passing the Courthouse. About a block away is a local Mexican restaurant that makes burritos that appeal to the Anglo palate. As I sit at one of the tables contemplating how this small Midwestern town is connected to Mexico and the immigration crisis, I conclude that whenever one nation builds roads into another nation to steal their cheap labor and natural resources, we should not be surprised when the inhabitants of those nations take those same roads and follow all that has been stolen from them.

DISCUSSION QUESTIONS

- What does the Midwest have to do with the immigration crisis? What role does corn play? Why is corn important to Mexico and Central America? What role does corn subsidies play in the current immigration debate? Why is Iowa corn growing crucial in preventing or curtailing corn subsidies?

- Explain NAFTA and its impact on the political and economic relationship between the U.S. and Mexico. What role has NAFTA played in creating the current immigration crisis? Has NAFTA helped the Mexican people? How has it or how has it not? Has it helped U.S. citizens? How has it or how has it not?

- What are *maquiladores*? How do they function within international trade? Why are *maquiladores* attractive to U.S. businesses? What impact do *maquiladores* have on the Mexican economy? On the U.S. economy? On the Mexican people? On U.S. citizens?

3

ON A TRAIL FIVE MILES FROM ARIVACA

WE ARRIVED AS THE sun was setting, forcing us to pitch our tents at dusk when it was hard to see what we were doing. I, however, was too tired and decided to sleep under the stars, an awesome sight of beauty far from the harsh city lights that usually obscure the view. The reason we arrived so late to the camp was due to our encounter with several migrants on the main road making their way northward. Driving south on Interstate 19 we existed at the Amado Road exit, then headed south on West Arivaca Road for about twenty-three miles towards the town of Arivaca. About half way to the town, we encountered about seven migrants. We stopped and provided them with some food and fresh water for their journey. Some asked how far was Tucson. They tell us that before beginning their northern journey, coyotes (smugglers) assured them that it would take a day to cross the mountains and another day to reach Tucson, Arizona. Like many, they crossed the desert unprepared, with insufficient water and food. For four days they crossed mountains, believing now that Tucson was less then a day's walk. When we responded the city was sixty miles to the north, their countenance fell. A few who were hopeless, defeated, and tired asked us to call the border patrol; they were giving up. We obliged their request and waited for the patrol vehicle to arrive. We witnessed as the migrants were quickly placed in what appears to be a covered dog-cage on the back of a pick-up truck.

Photographer: Vincent De La Torre

The migrants were well treated, mainly because we were present. For many migrants, the courteous conduct we witnessed is seldom offered. We have collected numerous testimonies of abuse during transportation of migrants by border patrol. The most common reported incidents include: 1) the absence of seat belts in Border Patrol and G4S/Wackenhut vehicles, 2) hazardous overcrowding to the point of creating a standing room only confined space, 3) high speed drives over rough terrain, especially when the vehicle is overcrowded, 4) intentional attempts to cause nausea among passengers by driving in circles, and 5) keeping vehicles at extreme temperatures. Javier, a teenager, reports that in 2009, after a beating by border agents, he was packed into a van with twenty other migrants as the agent recklessly drove the van all the while turning up the heat to maximum.[1]

One out of every ten migrants report some sort of physical abuse while in custody, and one in four report verbal abuse.[2] Patrol agents have been known to kidnap and rape the undocumented, including brown girls as young as fourteen years old.[3] Agents have beaten individuals, like Jose Gutierrez Guzman, into a comatose state.[4] At times, such abuses lead to death. As previously mentioned, between 2010 and (March) 2015, it is estimated that at least thirty-nine individuals were killed by the border patrol. They include Valerie Munique Tachiquin-Alvarado (thirty-two), a mother of five who, in a residential San Diego suburb, suffered fourteen gunshot wounds by a plain-clothed Border Patrol Agent.[5] Since 2014, the Border Patrol has been involved in more fatal shootings than perhaps any other U.S. law enforcement agency, developing a reputation for abuse and corruption. On average, between 2005 and 2012, one border agent was arrested each and every single day for misconduct.[6]

And yet, as James Wong, the Border Patrol's internal affairs investigator observed, "Not a single Border Patrol agent for the last eight years has been disciplined for excessive use of force. With a workforce that large, that's amazing." Wong continued by noting, "You go pull the stats on any medium-size municipal police force, pull the stats

---

1. No More Deaths, *A Culture of Cruelty,* 26–27.

2. The Center for Latin American Studies, *In the Shadow,* 24.

3. Ortiz, "Agent Sexually Assaults Family."

4. https://www.youtube.com/watch?v=xomI5NKo1gc.

5. https://www.youtube.com/watch?v=6wV_GMUq2aY&list=PLPWoddSADS1w1ZiM2ep83ExlVQJAwN3mn.

6. Graff, "Green Monster."

on the NYPD. At any given time, they'll have all sorts of excessive force investigations." Rather than dealing with abuse and corruption, during the first year of the Obama administration, the Border Patrol leadership was directed to change its definition of "corruption" to underrepresent the number of incidents.[7]

Once the border patrol vehicles departed with their human cargo, we continued our journey to the humanitarian camp outside Arivaca, a small town with about 700 residence comprised of about three blocks located eleven miles north of the Mexican border. We stopped at Virginia's Rancherita Food Truck for a quick bite of authentic tacos, aware that for the rest of our time at camp, the food served would be somewhat bland. Only the bottle of Kahlua brought by one of No More Death's organizers makes the camp meals tolerable. Before reaching the northern entrance to Arivaca we turn eastward, passing the Border Patrol station on our right until the paved road ends. We continue our snail-pace journey for a little over five miles southeast on a dirt road with multiple potholes. One gets the feel of what it must be like to ride a bronco, as all the contents, including the individuals aboard, are tossed back and forth. I cannot fathom what it would be like to be a migrant in the back of a border patrol vehicle, without a seatbelt, as the driver travels full speed. Right before the camp there is a dry ravine we cross. If a rainstorm blows through, this ravine becomes a raging river in minutes, making crossing impossible. Many such ravines exist in these isolated lands and many migrants have drowned when caught unaware by rushing waters. It takes awhile to comprehend that a major cause of migrant's deaths is drowning in a desert.

On the edge of the property owned by Byrd Baylor—an award-winning author of children's books and an

7. Ibid.

essayist—some land was offered to set up a No More Death's camp in 2004. No More Death is a humanitarian organization, operating as a decentralized coalition of diverse faith and community groups. The decentralized structure is itself a strategy designed to create difficulties for the authorities to target any one particular leader. Embracing a moral imperative that transcends human-made borders, No More Death provides direct medical and humanitarian aid to migrants crossing the desert in accordance with international laws what the U.S. purports to abide by.

Our commitment to stand in solidarity with the alien among us leads us to a camp that is literally located in the middle of nowhere, a desolate space close to the trails of hope and terror migrants traverse. Why would any rational person travel on such unforgiving terrain where they might die in the process? They are pushed to these hostile lands because of our government's official strategy known as Operation Gatekeeper. Operation Gatekeeper is a 1994 policy devised during the Clinton Administration in response to the unprecedented disruption to Mexico's small business and rural sectors caused by the economic liberalization brought about with the enactment of NAFTA.

One year before North American Free Trade Agreement was ratified, the General Accounting Office (GAO) predicted that implementing NAFTA would have the immediate consequence of an increase migration flow from Mexico. According to the GAO report: "the flow of illegal aliens across the southwest border is expected to increase during the next decade because Mexico's economy is unlikely to absorb all of the new job seekers that are expected to enter the labor force."[8] The report understood that the devastating impact NAFTA would have on the Mexican

8. U.S. General Accounting Office, "North American Free Trade Agreement."

economy and labor market would trigger an increase in immigration to the U.S. Then INS Commissioner Doris Meissner, when testifying before Congress in November 1993 about the short- and medium-term impacts of NAF-TA recognized that its ratification "will require strengthening our enforcement efforts along the border, both at and between ports of entry."[9]

Operation Gatekeeper was based on an earlier large-scale operation employed in El Paso, Texas known as Operation Hold-the-Line (originally called Operation Blockade), the first coordinated crackdown of undocumented immigration that began on September 19, 1993 at the U.S. side of the Bridge of the Americas (colloquially known as Cordova Bridge and/or Free Bridge). A few months after implementing operation Hold-the-Line, NAFTA went into affect on January 1 1994, and nine months later in September, Operation Gatekeeper was initiated.

Originally, border enforcement was a response to the U.S. implementation of its first immigration exclusion laws that targeted Asians in the 1880s. As early as 1904, no more than seventy-five agents from the U.S. Immigration Service patrolled the U.S. borders with Canada and Mexico looking for Asians attempting to enter the U.S. Finally, in the 1920s, Congress created a force to patrol the nation's unguarded borders. Since its creation, this agency has always suffered from bureaucratic neglect due to understaffing and underfunding.

During the Great Depression, up to one million Mexican immigrants and U.S. born citizens with Mexican ancestry were rounded up and deported in an attempt to reduce welfare rolls and create jobs for Anglos. A similar immigration policy occurred in 1954, when the Border Patrol engaged in its first large scale Mexican deportation

9. Nevins, "How High."

initiative callded Operation Wetback (political correctness was obviously not in vogue). It mattered little that among the 1.3 million Latinxs deported, some were documented. Those born in the U.S. were deported for the crime of looking Latinx. Although sporadic deportations of the undocumented occurred since then, it wasn't until the 1990s, with Operation Hold-the-Line, that a more systematic approached was implemented as a response to NAFTA. Anti-immigrant sentiments correspond to the downward mobility faced by many middle-class Euroamericans due to the globalization of the economy. Rather than holding economic elites responsible for the upward transfer of wealth, the immigrant became a scapegoat and was presented as a threat. Those blamed for the ills of society necessitate deportation, then and now, based on who looked like a Latinx—a disturbing trend because all Latinxs are first seen as not belonging, as foreign and thus in need of proving if they really belong.

How then do you prevent desperate people from risking everything, people who are highly motivated to find work in the U.S. in order to feed and cloth the families they are leaving behind? The premise upon which Operation Gatekeeper was based was a policy of "prevention through deterrence." In an August 1, 2001 letter to the U.S. Senate Committee on the Judiciary, Richard M. Stana of the U.S. General Accounting Office wrote that the ultimate goal of Operation Gatekeeper was "to make it so difficult and costly for aliens to attempt illegal entry that fewer individuals would try."[10] Making it costly means more than simply a financial expense; deterrence is also achieved through the loss of life. Some migrants die traversing dangerous terrain, but that is fine, because their deaths will deter others from attempting the hazard crossing. The death of brown

10. Stana, *INS Southwest Border Strategy,* 1.

migrant bodies was not some unforeseen consequence of Operation Gatekeeper, but acceptable "collateral damage." And while migrants always faced hazards when crossing the border prior to the implementation of Operation Gatekeeper, migrant deaths were rare.

The horrific death of migrants became an integral component of the "prevention through deterrence" policy. Even after decades where no empirical evidence exists that any migration was actually deterred, we continue with a policy where desperate people of color are placed into life-threatening situations so as to protect safe spaces for Euroamericans. Not since the days of Jim and Jane Crow do we have an official policy that relies on the death of people with a certain skin hue to deter others with a similar hue from committing similar actions.

If the hope was to deter migration, then Operation Gatekeeper has been a total failure according to the government's own assessments. No significant decrease in the number of unauthorized crossings since the start of Operation Gatekeeper has ever been reported. Rather than a decrease in the flow of unauthorized border crossing, the presence of undocumented immigrants has substantially increased from about 8.4 million in 2000 to about 11.3 million in 2015. And yet, the Border Patrol were reporting success due to lower apprehensions of undocumented immigrants; but allegations made by the Border Patrol Union suggest agents were encouraged to underreport numbers to create the allusion of effectiveness.[11] While it makes sense that a reduction of migrant crossing occurred in well patrolled sectors, particularly in urban areas, there exists no empirical evidence whatsoever that an overall reduction of undocumented crossings has occurred along the border.

11. McIntire Peters, "Up Against the Wall."

Although the illusion of controlled borders was constructed, the sad reality is that despite brown bodies perishing, no one was deterred. The reality is more deaths on the border since the implementation of Operation Gatekeeper. According to Bruce Anderson, forensic anthropologist for the Pima County Office of the Medical Examiner in Tucson, "Less people are coming across but a greater fraction of them are dying."[12] Even the U.S. Government Accounting Office recognizes Operation Gatekeeper for creating a humanitarian crisis.[13] It is difficult, if not impossible to determine how many people have actually perished attempting to cross the border. Seldom are any of these deaths reported by the news media. Nonetheless, it is estimated that five preventable deaths occurs every four days on the border,[14] deaths that remains invisible to the public consciousness. Although the Border Patrol estimates that about 6,000 have perished on the U.S.-Mexican border between 1998 and 2015;[15] the fact remains that we have no clue as to how many are actually dying. Part of the problem is that we lack any uniform or centralized database for counting the dead, identifying the dead, recovering the remains of the dead, determining the causes of death, burial of the dead, or the notification of the next of kin.

To complicate matters, whatever official numbers exists on how many are dying in our backyard, they are grossly underrepresented. According to an investigative report conducted by the *Tucson Citizen*, the Border Patrol undercounted border deaths by as much as 43 percent, a charge also made by the U.S. Government Accounting

12. Santos and Zemansky, "Arizona Desert Swallows Migrants."

13. Rubio-Goldsmith, et al., *"Funnel Effect" and Recovered Bodies,* 30.

14. Santos and Zemansky, "Arizona Desert Swallows Migrants."

15. Aguirre, "Deaths in the Desert."

Office.[16] Even if correct numbers were tallied, many still go uncounted, like those perishing on the Mexican side of the border, or those who do make it to the U.S. side but are never found due to remote and inaccessible terrain, or others whose remains are scattered due to predatory desert animals. The desert is very efficient in cleaning itself. In 2009, a joint research report conducted by the ACLU of San Diego and Imperial Counties with Mexico's National Human Rights Commission estimated that in the first fifteen years of Operation Gatekeeper, about 5,600 migrants died as direct result of our deadly deterrence policies. This averages to about one death a day, of which 7 to 11 percent of those who perish are children.[17]

Complicating the ability to obtain official numbers is the policy that Border Patrol only counts the bodies that they recover, ignoring those bodies found by humanitarian organizations like ours, or local authorities who are usually the first responders when called. Brown bodies are so devalued that they are not worth the effort of being properly counted. One body not counted—which is considered a (no)body by official authorities because it was not recovered by the Border Patrol—but nonetheless a somebody in the eyes of God, is Josseline Jamileth Hernández Quinteros, a fourteen-year-old Salvadorian girl heading to *el norte* to reunite with her mother. A petite brown girl at five feet and weighting about a hundred pounds with deep black eyes and hair, Josseline traveled over two thousand miles northward with her then ten-year-old brother.

The family has been separated for too long. The children lived with relatives as their mother Sonia worked as an undocumented immigrant in Los Angeles, California, and

---

16. LoMonaco, "Many Border Deaths Unlisted"; U.S. Government Accounting Office, "Illegal Immigration," 14.

17. Jimenez, *Humanitarian Crises,* 8, 28.

her father Santos, also undocumented, lived in Maryland. Trusting adults she knew, Sonia arranged to have her children join them on the trek northward. The trip was arduous: little food, sleeping whenever shelter could be found, hiking mountains, crossing deserts, jumping walls and fences, and constantly playing a cat and mouse game first with the Mexican *federales* and then with the U.S. *migra*. A coyote was paid thousands of dollars to guide the group across the international border, at the small-unincorporated border community of Sasabe, the least utilized port of entry. Once across, they only had a twenty-mile hike to Interstate 19 where a vehicle would pick them up and transport them deep into the U.S.

It was late January in 2008, and the weather was cold and damp with temperatures in the 50s, dropping to near freezing during the long nights. One of the ironies is that people can freeze to death in the Sonora Desert. Josseline must have been cold because she was wearing all of her clothes. She slipped her sweatpants, emblazoned with the word "Hollywood" on the rear, over her jeans, wore her two jackets, one of which was lined in pink, and wore her bright green sneakers. Not only was she cold, she was also tired. She had been traveling for weeks. For the last few days, she walked on the open trails, sleeping on the damp ground. Worse than being cold and tired, she became ill and started vomiting. By the time the migrants arrived to Cedar Canyon, she was simply unable to continue. Maybe she was dehydrated, or maybe she drank water from one of the cattle troughs that turns putrid when exposed to the elements. Some migrants have told me that out of desperation, they drank their own urine. Regardless, Josseline's retching weakened her, making it impossible for her to stand up, let alone keep up with the group.

The group had to maintain their fast pace if they hoped to catch the awaiting ride. Worse, if they stayed with the ill child, they risked being caught by the Border Patrol. Josseline was left behind. She was assured that the authorities would soon detect her presence. Her younger brother insisted on staying with his older sister, but she demanded that he continue the journey and be reunited with their mom. He was pulled away wailing and screaming while Josseline was left alone in the dark. That night, temperatures dropped to 29 degrees. It wasn't until the boy made it to his mom's embrace that the alarm was sounded.[18] The family contacted the Salvadoran consul in Nogales who in turn contacted border human rights organizations. Flyers were made and several volunteer patrols went out looking for Josseline.

About three weeks later, a group of four volunteers were on a water patrol in Cedar Canyon, a stretch of land that few traverse. Like us, they too were dropping off water, food, blankets, shoes and socks along some remote and isolated migrant trails. They heard about the missing girl but did not participate in the search, believing more good might come from placing life-giving supplies in the desert. They were making their way to a remote ridge where several migrant trails converge, believing that leaving supplies at this spot might do the most good. Walking up the side of the canyon for about twenty minutes, Dan Millis, who was spending a year working with No More Deaths, noticed fairly bright green shoes. He began to yell the familiar phrase "*Tenemos aqua, comida, somos de la iglesia*"—we have water and food, we are with the church. But before the second syllable left his month, he noticed that the owner of those shoes was not moving. She was lying on a rock, obscured by shrubbery, with her hands close to her head and her green sneakers in water gathered on the stone's crevice. Upon noticing her

18. Regan, *Death of Josseline*, ix–xii.

teeth, he realized she was dead. Because they contacted the local sheriff and not the Border Patrol, Josseline's body was not counted among the Border Patrol's tally.

Every time I have spoken to Dan Millis about that day, he remains shaken. Her body was so effected by the elements that a DNA test had to be conducted to confirm her identity. "How can I take solace," Millis asks,

> when finding a dead body in the desert is a regular occurrence in the U.S.? These deaths reveal the racism and inhumanity that is consuming our country. How can we feel secure when our neighbors are being rounded up as scapegoats in our own communities far from the border? How can anyone feel comforted when a kangaroo court called "Operation Streamline" is forcing poor and hungry people to beg a judge for forgiveness for their "crime" of trying to feed their families, or face jail time and criminal records? U.S. border policy is designed to neglect, berate, scapegoat, humiliate, torture, and kill innocent people. Let's change it. Now, goddammit![19]

Two months after the grisly discovery, a mass was conducted on the spot of her death and a cross was erected in her memory. Something is terribly wrong when a teenager perishes in the wealthiest country ever known to humanity due to the elements.

19. Millis, "Testimony from a Border Activist," 21–25.

Photographer: Vincent De La Torre

Prior to Operation Gatekeeper, nearly 25 percent of all border crossings nationwide occurred in the urban sections of the San Diego corridor.[20] The main danger that existed was getting caught and immediately deported, usually on the same day due to a "catch and release" policy. Under "catch and release," undocumented border crossers from Mexico would "voluntarily" sign a removal agreement that would authorize immediate expatriation without a court hearing and with no preclusion to future legal entry. Non-Mexicans would often be released within the U.S. while awaiting a court hearing for removal. The primary purpose of the Border Patrol was less in preventing northward migration to work the fields, and more on ensuring the return to Mexico after the harvest.

Upon ratifying NAFTA, and the consequence of increasing migration numbers, Operation Gatekeeper's strategy became the disruption of the northerly flow of brown bodies, beginning in the San Diego area. Shifting migration traffic away from urban areas by militarizing the border and building impregnable walls simply meant migrants undertook greater risk of injury or death crossing mountains,

20. Stana, *INS Southwest Border Strategy*, 5.

deserts, and rivers far from where the fence ended. Most were pushed toward 120,000 square miles of Sonora Desert or over the mountains north of Tecate. The shift of immigrant traffic to desolated areas had negative impacts on small communities like Arivaca. Local officials were not told of the Immigration and Nationalization Service (INS) policies, leaving such towns unprepared for an onslaught of traffic that crossed over private ranchland. Ranchers have incurred economic losses in the form of cut fences which allowed their livestock to get loose, ruined grazing fields due to heavy foot traffic, ecological damage due to trash being left behind, death of livestock that swallow the migrant's discarded plastic bottle caps, and/or stolen farm tools. Additionally, destruction of pristine areas in wildlife refuge and the overall environmental degradation can be attributed to the increase in foot traffic, and more significantly, the increase in Border Patrol presence.

Part of the militarization of the border includes the expansion of the Border Patrol that nearly doubled in size during the peak years of Operation Gatekeeper (1995 through 1999), from about 4,200 agents prior to the ratification of NAFTA to 8,200 five years later.[21] After 9/11, INS was disbanded and border security fell under the authority of the newly minted Department of Homeland Security. By 2011, the number of agents again doubled to 17,535 (not including the additional 6,000 National Guard troops deployed to the border as part of Operation Jump Start between 2006 and 2008, nor the 1,200 troops deployed in 2010), capping at about 21,000 in 2012.[22] Between 2011 and 2013, the U.S. government was allocating $3.5 billion

21. U.S. Department of Justice Office of the Inspector General, "Inspection of the Influx."

22. Lydgate, *Assembly-Line Justice,* 7; Lacey, "Border Deployment Will Take Weeks"; Sheldon, "Operation Streamline," 93.

per year for border security (spending more than the combined budgets of the ATF, DEA, FBI, NYPD, Secret Service, and the U.S. Marshals). Since 9/11, the U.S. has spent over $100 billion on border and immigration control, providing Border Patrol with the largest law enforcement air force in the world, equivalent to the size of Brazil's. Eighty-five percent of all border patrol agents are stationed along the U.S. southwestern border with Mexico.[23] Such rapid growth came at the cost of poor training and lack of proper field experience, as noted in a 2007 General Accounting Report.[24] Today, Customs and Border Protection has more agents authorized to carry a weapon and make arrests than any other federal law enforcement agency.

In the midst of this unforgiving and desolate land, surrounded by trails containing terror for those who traverse them, circled by an army of border patrol agents, we make camp. The camp has a medical tent that provides life-saving procedures to desperate people. I have witnessed individuals in camp with bloody blisters as big around as baseballs on both of their feet, unable to walk. A blister or a sprained ankle, common occurrences, can mean a death sentence as the group moves on, leaving the injured persons to fend for themselves.

Life at the humanitarian camp is, to say the least, primitive. With no running water, we begin our day with a simple breakfast after the use of a crude but effective latrine. Because of the August heat, we head for the wilderness in the early morning and the late afternoon, taking a siesta during the hottest hours of the day. It is madness to walk the trails during this time. Migrants recognize this and mostly travel at night, when its dark and hard to see, where some have even fallen into canyons, either hurting themselves or

23. Sheldon, "Operation Streamline," 92; Graff, "Green Monster."
24. Government Accounting Office, "Border Patrol."

losing their lives. Separating ourselves into small groups, we head out to trails that we believe will have migrant activity. As our group drives to the trailhead located in the Coronado National Forest by Lake Arivaca, about five miles east of town, we pass a tall nonfunctioning-monitoring tower on the right side of the road.

This tower is part of SBInet Surveillance, better known as the "virtual fence." High tech surveillance is employed to compensate for a lack of personnel or physical barriers in remote areas, specifically over a 28-mile stretch of the Arizona border. Through the use of radar, sensors, and cameras, the virtual fence was designed to detect migrant movement, but unfortunately, like the two earlier programs (Integrated Surveillance Intelligence System and America's Shield Initiative) that were scrapped for mismanagement and equipment failure, SBInet failed—unable to distinguish between a person and rain. Although the program was a colossal loss for the American taxpayers who are now the owners of tall towers in the desert that accomplish no purpose whatsoever, the $1.6 billion spent on the program was a windfall for Boeing who was awarded the contract.[25]

We arrive at the start of our trail and head up into the foothills, walking along a ravine, and climb through the canyons to leave food and water. Even though we are rested, fed, and hydrated, walking the trails are difficult and brutal. The saw grass is taller than me, and I stand six feet tall. It is called saw grass for a reason. Due to the heat, I made the mistake of wearing shorts and a t-shirt this day. Within minutes, the grass saws into my skin, leaving multiple scratches, as if I was on the losing side of a fight with a gang of cats. This stretch of terrain will witness daytime

25. Government Accounting Office, "Secure Border Initiative"; "Electronic Privacy Information Center"; "Surveillance at Our Border"; Shulz, "More High-Tech Setback."

temperatures exceeding 115 degrees Fahrenheit, higher during summer months. By nightfall, temperatures can drastically drop posing a risk of hypothermia. Other dangers include rattlesnake bites, falling into canyons where bodies have been retrieved, and of course, dying of dehydration. As we struggle on these trails, we are aware that the Tucson sector is the deadliest corridor on the border.

Not long ago I spoke with Angel, an undocumented man who made it to Tucson and is now living in the shadows of privilege. He recounted how on the second day after starting his desert trek with only two one-gallon jugs of water, he stumbled and dropped the jugs losing his precious commodity. Desperate, he kept walking. "But God is always with you," Angel told me, "later on . . . on the third day we found several jugs of water, and also some food, in the afternoon we found it." For those of us who have placed this precious commodity on migrant trails, it is encouraging and satisfying to know that this simple act of providing the necessities of life might actually save a life. And yet, as we walk pass water jugs we have left the previous day, I was puzzled to see that several were destroyed, some slashed with pocket knives.

One of our companions on the trails this day informs me that the Border Patrol have been known to destroy the water jugs. At first, I refused to believe the accusation, chalking it up to overzealous activist propaganda. After all, when addressing the humanitarian crisis caused by a large influx of women and children in 2014, Border Patrol Commissioner R. Gil Kerlikowske declared: "Our agency and the Department of Homeland Security have mobilized to address this situation in a way consistent with our laws and our American values."[26] I was inclined to believe

26. Official U.S. Customs and Border Protection website: http://www.cbp.gov/border-security/humanitarian-challenges#.

Commissioner Kerlikowske, unable to imagine the type of person who would destroy a life source whose absence could bring about the death of another human being, as was the case with Josseline.

It was not until I witnessed, with my own eyes, the Border Patrol destroying the water jugs left by our humanitarian organization that I became radicalized. Volunteers from the No More Death camp set up and camouflaged a motion-sensitive video camera facing water jugs left behind for the migrants. The first scene shows a cow, mooing, while strolling by the water jugs. The second scene shows three border patrol agents walking by as a female officer kicks over the jugs of water. The third and last scene shows a group of migrants walking by observing the destroyed water jugs.[27] As powerful as this clip was, more damning is a clip shot by Kevin Riley who was approached by agent David Kermes after he and his patrol left water on the trail. Border Patrol Agent Kermes approaches the group asking if they left this litter on the trail. He immediately begins to pour the water on the ground as he dares the group of volunteers to admit they were the ones who placed the water.[28] The No More Death patrol remains silent knowing that volunteers from our camp have in the past been charged with littering for leaving water on these trails.[29] In July 2009, forty humanitarian volunteers entered Buenos Aires National Wildlife Refuge (immediately west of Arivaca) to place water jugs when temperatures exceed 110 degrees, only to be ticketed for littering.[30] Ironically, we are the ones who pick up and bring back to camp as much garbage left on the trail that we could carry to properly dispose of the waste, empty water

27. https://www.youtube.com/watch?v=za_Tmt9rSGI.

28. https://www.youtube.com/watch?v=ZL1N-asKkOg.

29. Jimenez, *Humanitarian Crises*, 43.

30. Ibid., 45.

bottles, plastic jugs, clothing, and other personal items. Agent Kermes looks directly into the camera with the hubris of knowing his actions will carry no consequences and exclaims, "You don't scare me."

We've been walking through the Coronado National Forest on this canyon trail for about an hour. My feet ache. In my backpack I am carrying four jugs of water, each weighting about eight to nine pounds. I also have a jug of water in each hand. The journey is difficult as we jump over barbed-wired fences and scramble over a twelve-foot wall of boulders. We walk by rotten slimy green buggy water in cattle ponds were migrants who, unable to find our water jugs, might be tempted out of desperation to drink. Already, I am exhausted, soaked in sweat and trying to conserve my own water. Along the trail we pass a shrine constructed within the crevice of a canyon ridge by migrant travelers, a reminder that even in the presence of the shadow of the valley of death, there are symbols of the Divine in the form of crosses, statues of saints, and prayer cards. As we slowly make our way, I yell at the top of my lungs: "*Tenemos comida, agua y medicinas. Estamos con la iglesia. No tengo miedo*—We have food, water and medicine. We are with the church. Do not be afraid." Migrants are usually afraid we might be the Border Patrol, or worse, one of the numerous vigilante groups patrolling and terrorizing the border. Our words are meant to encourage migrants to reveal themselves and receive the lifesaving supplies we carry. On this day, we do not come across any migrants.

However, another one of our patrols that day walking on a different trail experienced a transcendent moment. This group of volunteers did not have among them a fluent Spanish speaker. They noticed in the distance some migrants, who upon spotting the volunteers on patrol, turned to run away. Our group begin to yell the customary phrase of having food, water, and medicine, and being with the church. The migrants misunderstood. Stopping in their tracks, they turned around and made their way back to our group. "We don't have much food or water," they said, "but what we do have, we'll share with you." These so-called "illegals" misheard the cry to offer assistance as a cry for help. Those who had so little were willing to share their meager resources with those of us who have so much.

We who profess Christianity are familiar with Jesus' admonishment to imitate the example of the Good Samaritan (Luke 10:29–37). On this day, the migrants who were quick to fill that role humbled those of us who went to the desert to be like the Good Samaritan. To be faithful to the parable of the Good Samaritan means we must care for all we find in the wilderness who are hungry, thirsty, and naked—regardless of documentation. To imitate the Good Samaritan and take a dying migrant found by the side of the road to our camp so as to bind their wounds and nurse them to recovery is a punishable offense (transporting undocumented immigrants) that can result in up to twenty years in prison and the confiscation of one's motor vehicle. Like the religious leaders who found justification for ignoring God's will, so too do our laws make it impossible to practice our faith, even as government officials routinely destroy the means by which life can be sustainable on this unforgiving land. Not wanting to romanticize the migrants, on this day, they were the ones that best exemplified the meaning of the Good Samaritan.

That afternoon we returned to camp to find a dozen mounted Border Patrol agents. We were detained as border agents debated charging us with aiding and abetting the undocumented. Harboring an undocumented immigrant is punishable by up to $250,000 fine and ten years in prison. A bale of marijuana was found in a remote section of the property and there was talk of arresting us for drug smuggling. Being that this discovery was news to us, we could only speculate that it was disposed of for later retrieval by a drug smuggling ring (which we doubted because the bale was full of worms and in unusable condition), or it might have been planted by those raiding our camp. To this day, we don't know. We were housing three migrants who stumbled into our camp, providing them with life-saving medical attention. Because they were in need, we never bothered to ask them for their immigration status. The border agents saw it differently. After several hours, they simply arrested our three "guests" and drove off. Not to sound trite, but we were left wondering if providing humanitarian aid has become a crime in this country.

DISCUSSION QUESTIONS

- Crossing the U.S. southern border is life threatening. What type of hazards does a migrant face? Why are they willing to risk their lives? If you were in a similar situation, would you risk your life? Is the U.S. complicit with creating these hazardous conditions? Why or why not?

- Is a "deterrent policy" effective? Humane? Why or why not? Explain the evolution of Operation Gatekeeper. Is this current immigration policy humane? Is it racist? How is the current policy assessed for effectiveness? Is it working? If so, should it be strengthened; if not, should it be abandoned as a failure? Can a person of faith support Operation Gatekeeper? Why or why not?

- Regardless of your views concerning immigration, how should U.S. law enforcement agents treat undocumented migrants who are arrested? Is their current treatment by Border Patrol a violation of basic human rights? Why or why not? What basic safeguards should be in place when dealing with the undocumented?

4

AT A TEA PARTY ANTI-IMMIGRANT PROTEST

"Howdy y'all, my name's Mike." Only when I was in my twenties and tried to assimilate to the dominant culture did I ever Anglicize my name, but with the raising of my consciousness, so too came a full embrace of my Latinx identity. Naming oneself is a crucial liberative step for any person accustomed to being named by others. Choosing Miguel, and pronouncing it correctly, is a revolutionary praxis that forces those accustomed to "English only" to deal with my presence, a reminder that I am not invisible. And yet, on this hot July 14th day in 2014, I entered this small community of about 3,600 residents and made the conscious decision to mask my identity. Trying to channel a Southern drawl (unsuccessfully I might add) picked up from years living in Kentucky, I approached the organizers of an anti-immigrant rally. I held deep concerns for my safety, fearing the use of my Spanish name in the midst of a crowd that was shouting insults at Latinx folks. A sign on the back of a pickup truck flat bed that read, "Impeach the Dictator—Go Home non-Yankees" failed to reassure my anxieties. I noticed other signs that read, "Return to Sender," "No Se Puede," "What about our Children?? Resourses [sic] to them!"

Photographer: Vincent De La Torre

According to the Border Patrol, about 55,420 family members have been apprehended at the U.S.-Mexican border from October 2013 through the end of June 2014, a near 500 percent increase over the same period during the previous year. These families were primarily comprised of women and children, mainly from Central America, who began their northern trek to escape the gang violence of their homelands. Additionally, 57,525 unaccompanied minors were detained by the end of that June creating a humanitarian crisis on the border.[1] Unlike most undocumented immigrants who try to avoid detection by the Border Patrol, these women and children, once within the United States, sought border agents. Rumors spread within their countries, specifically Guatemala, Honduras, and El Salvador, that if they made it to the United States, they would be allowed to stay. Instead, these women and children were

1. "Arizona Protestors Mistake Busload."

placed in inadequate detention centers as the government tried to figure out what to do with them.

But rumors were not limited to those south of the border. In the small town of Oracle, located about thirty-six miles north of Tucson, rumors began to swirl that forty to sixty Central American undocumented children were going to be bussed to Sycamore Canyon Academy, a treatment facility located in the Catalina Mountains serving troubled teen boys, a thirty-minute winding southeastern scenic drive from Oracle. Oracle's Sheriff Babeu played a key role in organizing the anti-immigrant protest, using social media and citing so-called "whistleblowers" at the Department of Homeland Security to rile up the local residents by playing on their fears. Babeu stated, "We already have our hands full fighting the drug cartels and human smugglers. We don't need unaccompanied juveniles from Central America being flown into Arizona, compliments of President Obama. Local residents have every right to be upset and to protest."[2] Ironically, although those at the rally were blaming Obama for the influx of children, it was then-President George W. Bush who signed the 2008 anti-trafficking law that requires the Border Patrol to turn over minors, within seventy-two hours, to the Department of Health and Human Services for processing.

Some critics of the sheriff's engagement in the anti-immigration movement raised concerns that he was inciting turmoil for political gain. Paul Babeu was once a rising star in the local Republican Party, serving as the co-chair of Romney's presidential campaign in Arizona and had aspirations of occupying a congressional seat. Unfortunately for him, he became embroiled in a scandal. Allegations surfaced from his former boyfriend—an undocumented

2. Holstege and Dale, "Protestors in Oracle"; "Arizona Residents Protest."

Mexican twenty-five years his junior—that Sheriff Babeu threatened him with deportation if their relationship ever became public.[3] In spite of the scandal, Babeu announced his run for the Congressional 1st District on October 12, 2015. As this book goes to press, he is one of seven candidates fighting for the Republican nomination in this district.

Based on the Sheriff's rumors of approaching undocumented immigrant children, an anti-immigrant rally was organized for that Tuesday. Several humanitarian groups appeared to show support for the immigrant minors, complete with "shielding angels" whose large wings attempted to block the racist signs of the anti-immigrant protestors from the children on the bus. What transpired was tense with anti-immigrant protestors shouting "Commies" to the humanitarian groups and some going so far as to spit on them. The number of protestors and anti-protestors swelled to about 130 (eighty white anti-immigrant and fifty multiethnic pro-immigrant). When a group of mariachi musicians showed up, the protestors shoved them.[4]

The anti-immigrant rally took shape after the sheriff informed Oracle resident Robert Skiba about the rumored federal plans of housing minors. Skiba, a possible Tea Partier as implied by the "Don't Tread on Me" baseball cap he wore during several television interviews, became the main organizer of the rally.[5] I spend my time at the rally speaking to Skiba, a gentleman in his late sixties wearing a white polo shirt and standing with others before a waving American flag. He assured me that they were prepared to use whatever peaceful means at their disposal to prevent

3. Snejana and Associated Press Reporter, *Daily Mail* (UK).

4. Dale, "Babeu Keeps Peace"; "Arizona Protestors Mistake Busload."

5. "Arizona Protestors Mistake Busload."

the buses carrying undocumented children from reaching their final destination. "This is sacred area to the people who use this canyon, and to dump these forty lawbreakers into our backyard is totally unacceptable and we plan to do everything in our power to stop it." The demonstrators, who were camped on Mount Lemon Road, the only route to Sycamore Canyon Academy, were influenced by a protest that occurred in Murrieta, California earlier in the month. In early July, residents of Murrieta, a city of about 107,000 about sixty miles west of Palm Springs California, blocked buses carrying immigrant children who where being taken to a Border Patrol facility for processing.

When I asked Skiba what exactly was his concern, he listed several items. He was afraid that these children were dangerous. "We don't know who these kids are. They show us pictures of nice kids playing ring-around-the-rosy. Is that the type of kids they're sending? We don't think so. Are they MS-13 [abbreviation for Mara Salvatrucha, an international criminal gang that originated in Los Angeles]? Are they gang-bangers?" The immigrant Other as criminal is a recurring rhetorical expression, ignoring FBI statistics showing border communities to be among the safest in the nation with no evidence of spillover violence from Mexico. Academic studies reveal immigrants commit crimes at lower rates than native born. In fact, a significant drop in cartel- and gang-related arrests along the Texas southern border was reported even as a 2014 surge of border crossings occurred. Besides, four out of five arrests for drug smuggling involved U.S. citizens, not immigrants.[6] Skiba also expressed concerned about diseases crossing the border, wondering if they had medical examinations. He was unaware that due to excellent medical services in these

6. Wilson, *Crime Data and Spillover Violence*, 1–3; *Immigration Policy Center*, 1–3; Ye Hee Lee, "Donald Trump's False Comments."

countries, Pima County Health Director Francisco Garcia wrote in a memorandum to the county administer that the unaccompanied children being transferred through Nogales posed no public health threat.[7]

For many at the rally, there is an unexamined assumption that undocumented immigrants are unfairly using up social services to which they are not entitled. Even former presidential hopeful and former Arkansas governor Mike Huckabee claimed that the solvency of Social Security and Medicare was under threat from "illegals, prostitutes, pimps, drug dealers, all the people that are freeloading off the system now."[8] The reality is that these so-called "illegals" are contributing to the solvency of Social Security. More than 3.1 million undocumented workers, using fake or expired social security numbers, contribute $13 billion annually into the system while only receiving $1 billion in return benefits. According to Stephen Goss, chief actuary of the Social Security Administration, the undocumented paid over $100 billion into the system between 2005 and 2014. Goss goes on to say, "You could say legitimately that had we not received the contributions that we have had in the past from undocumented immigrants . . . that would of course diminish our ability to be paying benefits for as long as we now can."[9] In addition, according to a fifty-state analysis by the Institute on Taxation and Economic Policy, 8.1 of the 11.4 million undocumented immigrants contributed more than $11.8 billion in state and local taxes in 2012.[10] One is left wondering if Governor Huckabee is simply ignorant of how Social Security and Medicare are kept afloat thanks

7. Holstege and Dale, "Protestors in Oracle Inspired."

8. Bazelon, "Unwelcome Return of 'Illegals.'"

9. Sakuma, "Undocumented Workers."

10. Gardner, et al., *Undocumented Immigrant State*, 1–2.

to the undocumented contributions; or, if he is disingenuously lying to create fear and garner votes.

The fear expressed by Skiba and other anti-immigrant protestors in Tea-Party-type rallies finds justification in the false statements of politicians designed to galvanize an angry constituency, upset that the white privilege that once undergirded their power and social position is being dismantled with what they dismiss as political correctness. No doubt these anti-immigrant protestors rejoiced when they heard Donald Trump announce his candidacy for the 2016 presidency with his now notorious phrase: "When Mexico sends its people, they're not sending their best. They're not sending you. They're not sending you. They're sending people that have lots of problems, and they're bringing those problems with us. They're bringing drugs. They're bringing crime. They're rapists. And some, I assume, are good people."[11]

Should we therefore be surprised when two Boston brothers, Scott and Steve Leader, urinated on and severely beat a homeless Latinx man citing Donald Trump immigration stance? "Donald Trump was right, all these illegals need to be deported," Scott Leader later told police. When Trump was told of the alleged assault committed in his name, he responded with, "it would be a shame . . . I will say that people who are following me are very passionate. They love this country and they want this country to be great again. They are passionate."[12]

Finally, buses of children arrived. Arizona Representative Adam Kwasman who was among the anti-immigrant protestors tweeted, "Bus coming in. This is not compassion. This is the abrogation of the rule of law."[13] Protestors rushed

11. Ye Hee Lee, "Donald Trump's False Comments."
12. DiNatale and Sacchetti, "South Boston Brothers."
13. "Arizona Protestors Mistake Busload."

to the buses with racist signs to confront the children and force them out of their community. The children in the bus were terrified as a violent mob approached them yelling insults. Unfortunately for all involved, the buses were carrying local children from the YMCA. When all is said and done, the protest comes to an end with no buses of undocumented children ever appearing; leading us to wonder, were any ever coming? After all, housing forty to sixty children out of 57,525 doesn't seem to make sense in attempting to meet an immediate need. According to Representative Raul Grijalva who contacted the Department of Health and Human Services, no buses were ever planned to arrive at this small community.[14]

As I stand in the midst of this anti-immigrant rally, I realize that no one is asking why are Salvadorians, Hondurans, and Guatemalans coming to the United States? Why are tens of thousands of unaccompanied children from these countries showing up on our doorsteps? In previous chapters we explored how Mexicans are taking the roads we built into their countries to extract, thanks to NAFTA, their cheap labor and resources. But why Central Americans? We have to ask why these children risk death to cross not one international border, but several. To reach the United States, they must first traverse the entire length of Mexico, a 1,950 mile walk from Guatemala-Mexico border to Brownsville, Texas. This does not take into consideration that for Hondurans and Salvadorans, they must also traverse the entire length of Guatemala. Of course, most don't walk the entire Mexican trek, but instead ride on top of a train, called *la bestia* ("the beast"), a treacherous ride where the migrant might fall off and either die under the wheels of the train or at best, lose a limb or two. Gangs patrol these trains, robbing the migrants of their meager possessions. Women and

14. Ibid.

young girls are the most vulnerable, facing rape and abuse. Before Central American migrants get to face the abusive practices of the U.S. Border Patrol, they must first survive the abusive practices of *los federales* of Mexico.

The reasons Central American migrants risk their lives and make this hazardous trek is rooted in the historical relationship between the U.S. and Central America. Contrary to the anti-immigrant rhetoric I heard at the Oracle rally, they do not come to deplete American social services. They attempt the perilous crossing because our foreign policy throughout the twentieth century has created an economic situation in their countries where they are unable to feed their families or keep their families safe. Throughout the twentieth century, the U.S. military provided and protected the freedom of U.S. corporations to build roads into developing Central American countries to extract, by brute force if necessary, their natural resources and cheap labor. They too come following what has been stolen. They come to escape the violence and terrorism our foreign policy unleashed in order to confiscate their resources and cheap labor. This changes the questions usually asked about these women and unaccompanied children. The real question we are faced with is not whether they should come, but ethically and morally, what responsibilities and obligations exist for the U.S. in causing the present immigration dilemma.

The reason why women and children are on our border in 2014 can be traced to almost 150 years ago. They are at our borders today due to bananas back then. Americans first experienced the taste of bananas during the 1876 Philadelphia Centennial Exposition. Because bananas require fourteen to twenty-three consecutive months of frost-free sunny weather to bear fruit, plants mainly flourish throughout the Caribbean basin. Lack of a transportation infrastructure meant most of the bananas exported northward would overripe before reaching U.S. ports. But the move from schooners to steamships, and the introduction of on-board cooling techniques established the feasibility of getting Central American bananas to U.S. markets. Two individuals, Lorenzo Dow Baker (a Cape Cod fishing captain) and Minor Keith (a ruthless Central America railroad builder), independently of each other, are credited with being the first to successfully transport bananas to the American consumer. By 1880, Baker and Keith, along with Andrew Preston (a Boston fruit merchant who with Baker owned a steamship fleet), joined forces to create the Boston Fruit Company. By 1899, Americans were consuming over sixteen million bunches a year, literally going bananas over bananas. Ten years later, the U.S. was flooded with bananas. That was also the year that Boston Fruit merged with United Fruit to create the notorious United Fruit Company, the largest banana company in the world, with plantations throughout Central America, South America, and the Caribbean.[15]

Around this time President Theodore Roosevelt started talking about "gun boat diplomacy" and "speaking softly but carrying a big stick." These policies laid the foundation for the development of today's multinational corporations. Roosevelt's foreign policy described how the full force of the U.S. military, specifically the Marines, was at the disposal of U.S. corporations, specifically the United Fruit Company, to protect their business interest. Nicknamed *El Pulpo*—"the Octopus"—because its tentacles extended into every power structure within Central America, the United Fruit Company was able to set prices, taxes, and employee treatment free from local government intervention. By 1930, the company had a 63 percent share of the banana market. Any nation in "our" hemisphere that attempted to

15. Jenkins, *Bananas*, 16–21.

claim their sovereignty to the detriment of U.S. business interests could expect the U.S. to invade and set up a new government (hence the term "banana republic"—coined in 1935 to describe servile dictatorships). It is no coincidence that the rise of U.S. banana consumption coincided with the rise of U.S. imperialist actions throughout the Caribbean Basin.

When Manuel Estrada Cabrera, the Guatemalan dictator, gave United Fruit free reign to own land so the company could grow bananas in 1901, the U.S. military made sure United Fruit Company's interests were well protected there. By the 1930s, the company held most of the land of Guatemala. Not only was Guatemala under the control of U.S. companies as a "banana republic," but so was every nation along the Caribbean Sea (along with several South American countries).

By the 1950s, 70 percent of the land in Guatemala was controlled by 2.2 per cent of the population, with only 10 percent of the land available to 90 percent of the mostly indigenous population. Jacobo Árbenz was eventually elected president through a free and open democratic election. He developed the Agrarian Reform Law to deal with the land injustices. However, he ran into one major problem. The United Fruit Company was a major holder of unused land. In 1953, the government appropriated a quarter of a million acres of the company's land, reimbursing the company the amount they declared the land was worth on their company's tax return—a figure that the company exceedingly undervalued. Angered, the United Fruit Company approached the U.S. government to protect their business interests.

A Central Intelligence Agency covert operation in 1954 orchestrated a *coup d'état*, overthrowing the democratically elected government of Árbenz and replacing it with the military dictatorship of Colonel Castillo Armas under the pretense that Árbenz was a communist. From the U.S. embassy, a disinformation campaign (through a hired public relation firm), a full-blown destabilization program, and the coordination of military support with a so-called rebel army of 150 men, coordinated the demise of Árbenz on behalf of United Fruit. Allen Dulles, the Deputy Director of the CIA and his brother, John Foster Dulles Secretary of State spearheaded the overthrow. Prior to their appointments in the Eisenhower Administration, both brothers did legal work for United Fruit through the law firm Sullivan and Cromwell, and sat on United Fruit's board of directors. Then Under Secretary of State, Bedell Smith, the point man who coordinated the U.S. government's efforts to overthrow Árbenz, became, in 1954, a director of Untied Fruit. For the first time, the U.S. government engaged in an intensive paramilitary and psychological campaign to overthrow a popular country with a political nonentity, a success that became the blueprint for all future CIA regime changes throughout Latin America and the world. Upon ousting Árbenz, Castillo Armas immediately returned so-called confiscated land to United Fruit. Of course Guatemala is not the only country where brutal dictators that would protect the business interests of U.S. corporations were installed.[16]

Following the ouster of Árbenz, the country was thrown into political chaos resulting in four decades of state terror marked with over 50,000 deaths, over 100,000 disappeared, and 626 village massacres. Throughout the twentieth century, eleven Caribbean countries experienced twenty-one U.S. military invasions and twenty-six covert CIA operations. During most of the twentieth century, no country would be allowed to determine who would serve

16. Striffler and Moberg, eds. *Banana Wars*, 63, 90, 193, 218.

as their leaders without the expressed permission of the U.S. ambassador to that country. The consequences resulting from these U.S.-installed "banana republics" were the creation of poverty, strife, and death. During the 1980s, U.S. foreign policies designed to safeguard established "banana republics" in Central America led to military conflicts in places like El Salvador, Honduras, and Guatemala. The reason women and children from those countries are on our borders today is directly linked to over a century of U.S. imperialism within their countries.

As I spoke with Skiba, I asked him what he thought might be the solution in dealing with these unaccompanied minors. He looked me straight in the eye and said that the answer was to move the U.S. international border to the south of Mexico and thus stop the Hondurans, Salvadorians and Guatemalans before they enter Mexico. I was intrigued by his comment, not sure if he was calling for the annexation of Mexico, or simply invade that sovereign nation to strengthen the security of their southern border. At first, I dismissed his comments as nativist; but the more I pondered on his words, the more his proposed solution became the plan of action realized by the United States.

Ironically, Skiba's solution was implemented by the same Obama administration to which he showed great disdain during our conversation. Starting the very month I was speaking with Skiba, Mexico, at the request and with the assistance of the U.S., began an unprecedented and ferocious crackdown of refugees fleeing Central America. The U.S. provided Mexico with tens of millions of dollars for the fiscal year that ended in September 2015 to stop these migrants from reaching the U.S. border. In a way, the U.S. outsourced the women and children refugee crisis. Starting in July 2014, Mexico redirected 300 to 600 immigration agents to its southernmost border, conducting over 20,000 raids on the freight trains upon which immigrants ride, and at the bus stations, hotels, and highways they traverse while on their northward journey. During the first seven months of fiscal 2015, Mexican authorities apprehended 92,889 Central Americans trying to reach the United States (more than the 70,448 apprehended by the U.S. during the same period).

The efforts of anti-immigrant rallies and groups is to foster sentiments responsible for borders throughout the United States. To live on the borders can literally mean living in the cities that are located along the artificial international line. According to the Census Bureau, approximately thirteen million American and Mexican residents live in the border areas separating these two nations. But the border cannot be limited to just one geographical reality—they also symbolize the existential location of all U.S. Latinxs, regardless of documentation. Those who succeeded in traversing the death-causing obstacles of the border and are disbursed throughout the fifty states still find themselves living on the borders. They live on the borders—on the borders between legitimacy and illegitimacy, the borders between economic class and poverty, the borders between acceptance and rejection, the border between life and death. We all are cognizant of the physical wall that demarks where the First and Third World collides signifying the clash between global power and forced underdevelopment; but few recognize the invisible wall that exists in every small community and metropolitan center designed to separate Latinxs from the rest of the dominant U.S. culture.

Most Latinxs (both undocumented and documented), regardless as to where they are located or how they or their ancestors found themselves in the United States, live on the borders. Borders separating Latinxs from others from the dominant culture exists in every state, every city, and almost every community, regardless as to how far away they may be from the physical wall. Borders are as real in Chicago, Illinois; Topeka, Kansas; or Saint Paul, Minneapolis, as they are San Diego, California; Nogales, Arizona; or El Paso, Texas. To be a U.S. Latinx is to constantly live on the border, that is, the border that separates privilege from disenfranchisement, that separates power from marginalization, and that separates whiteness from brownness. To live on the border, whether in close proximity to the physical wall on the international line or the invisible walls throughout the U.S. means separation from the benefits and the fruits society has to offer those who contribute to the general welfare. Exclusion mainly occurs because Latinxs are conceived by the dominant Euroamerican culture as not belonging, as perpetual "illegals." For example, why do we call those from Latin America living in the U.S. "migrants"—a term that has come to signify "less than," a term that connotes uneducated, unskilled, uninformed? And yet, when Euroamericans live in Latin America, as do many retirees hoping to stretch their social security benefits, they are referred to as "expats," which connotes adventure and savvy. Even though both have migrated for economic reasons, expats are reserved for those of European descent. Using different terms betrays our biases. What would happen if we started calling Euroamericans living abroad migrants and the undocumented at our borders expats?

Not surprising, because many Latinxs are seen as inferior due to their mixture (specifically racial mixture), most cluster in the lower stratum of the economy, receiving the lowest weekly wages of any major group in the labor market. According to U.S. governmental statistics, Latinxs are more likely to be victims of crime than non-Latinxs; more likely to serve longer prison sentences if convicted of a crime; more likely to live with pollution; have disproportionately lower levels of educational attainment; and are less likely to carry health insurance. Even those of us who discuss immigration as Latinx scholars, do so from the social location of residency or citizenship with a false security that comes with occupying a space north of the border.

The reality of brownness in America today became obvious during a routine October 2015 court procedure concerning a Latinx motorist pulled over for driving while under the influence of being brown. Mauro Martinez, a Guatemalan, was pulled over for allegedly speeding by Oldham County Police in Kentucky. Missing from the citation was any indication as to how fast Martinez was driving. During an exchange with defense counsel and District Judge Diana Wheeler, Assistant County Attorney John K. Carter argued that the "issue is he [Martinez] was stopped because he was Hispanic." In the court video he affirmed, "That's probable cause." Only after the video became public did Carter vehemently deny he was referring to Martinez's ethnicity.[17] The anti-immigrant rhetoric undergirding most of the immigration conversation makes all Latinxs suspect. Being Latinx, in and of itself, is probable cause. The government, along with racist segments of the general public, participates in violence (physical and/or institutionalized).

Nicholas Hausch, an eighteen-year-old from Long Island, illustrates the dangers of being Latinx in America today. He pleaded guilty to second-degree attempted assault as a hate crime for the stabbing of thirty-seven-year-old Ecuadorean named Marcelo Lucero. Hausch and a companion confessed to going out that evening to play a popular game known as "beaner hopping." Before the New York State Supreme Court, Hausch described the game "beaner hopping" to a packed courtroom. "It's when you go

17. Bailey, "Prosecutor Slammed."

out and you look for a Hispanic to beat up."[18] Hausch's action are not the exception to the rule, but a growing trend of violence toward Latinxs that correlates with the increase of anti-Latinx hate speech, as uttered during the Oracle rally. We should not be surprised that according to FBI statistics, anti-Latinx hate crimes increased 40 percent between 2003 and 2007,[19] the same period that anti-immigration started to be used as a wedge issue by politicians to garner votes for elections.

Prior to this rise in Latinx hate crimes, the normative condescending construct of Latinxs was that they were from a noble race of hard workers. Now they are dangerous lazy criminals set on violating and destroying the American way of life. As former Republican Congressman and 2008 presidential candidate Tom Tancredo succinctly put it, "Many who enter the country illegally are just looking for jobs, but others are coming to kill you, and you, and me, and my children, and my grandchildren."[20] The anti-immigrant rhetoric may be aimed against non-documented Latin Americans crossing the border; but in the minds of the general population, distinctions between a Latin American and a U.S. Latinx may remain unnoticeable. Among the last things the properly documented Ecuadorean Lucero heard before dying were racial epithets about him being Mexican. Clearly, among those expounding anti-Latinx sentiments, not only do all Latinxs look alike (Mexicans and Ecuadoreans) but they also don't belong (undocumented or documented).

As I walked among the anti-immigrant protestors reading their signs and hearing them express their views about brown people, I was left with a sickening feeling that in their words and deeds, brown lives don't matter. A

18. Fernandez, "Teenager Testifies About Attacking Latinos."

19. Schiavocampo, "Anti-Latino Hate Crimes."

20. McLean, "Immigration's Tancredo's Top Topics."

"post-racist society" is a term that has been much tossed around of late. Still, in cities throughout the United States it is common to hear race-based, anti-immigrant, anti-Latinx rhetoric. They come to use our services and to take advantage of what we have to offer are common refrains. This anti-immigrant rhetoric is not designed to solely demonize and marginalize the undocumented. The intent is also to demonize and marginalize documented Latinxs.

How the conversation is constructed betrays Euro-centric biases and ethnic discriminations. For example, the use of the term "illegal" is not a neutral word; it connotes criminality—that those who are illegal are somehow inherently bad, if not evil. In 2005, Republican political strategist Frank Luntz, who gave us the phrase "death tax," and helped write the Contract with America, proclaimed that when discussing undocumented migrants, "Always refer to people crossing the border illegally as 'illegal immigrants'— NOT as 'illegals.'"[21] But do we call a driver who is driving without a license an illegal driver? Or do we call a taxpayer who fails to file his documents on time an illegal citizen? Of course not. Not having proper documentations, either as a driver or filing one's taxes, does not make the person an inherent criminal. The reason migrants without proper documentation are called illegal has nothing to do with their character, or their moral framework; they are illegal because those in power have the legislative authority to impose their definitions on the least of society.

Language is not the only tool used to normalize anti-immigrant biases. Racist groups are also engaged in the discourse that perpetuate misinformation to legitimize anti-immigrant biases, as is the case with the Minutemen Project. The Minutemen Project recruits civilian volunteers to guard the U.S.-Mexican border from what they call

21. Bazelon, "Unwelcome Return."

"illegal" immigration, claiming the government has failed to secure the borders properly. According to Jim Gilchrist, president and co-founder of the organization, "We are not going to the border to invade anyone. We are going there to stop an invasion."[22] The Minutemen Project has similar goals and uses similar rhetoric in their call as the 1977 civilian border watch project organized by Grand Dragon Tom Metzger, Imperial Wizard David Duke, and Louis Beam of the Knights of the Ku Klux Klan. The racist rhetoric of the Minutemen can easily be detected in the pronouncements of Chris Simcox, co-founder of the Minutemen Project and the former president of the Minuteman Civil Defense Corps. According to Simcox, "These people don't come here to work. They come here to rob and deal drugs. . . . We need the National Guard to clean up our cities and round them up . . . [Mexicans and Central Americans] have no problem slitting your throat and taking your money or selling drugs to your kids or raping your daughter and they are evil people."[23] Sadly, it is he who, as of this writing, is standing trial for sexually assaulting three young girls, including his daughter.[24] Anti-immigrant sentiments justify abuses. Since 1999, migrants have filed complaints against the Minutemen Project reporting being shot at, bitten by dogs, hit with flashlights, kicked, taunted, and unlawfully imprisoned.[25]

The ethnic discrimination, abuse, and death brown bodies constantly and consistently face is alarming. And while the national narrative mainly focuses on the plight of African Americans, the social location of Latinxs seldom pierces the U.S. conscious. Much has been said concerning

22. Parker, "Minutemen Project Beginning."

23. Holthouse, "Arizona Showdown."

24. Lemons, "Former Minuteman Leader."

25. ACLU, *Creating the Minutemen.*

black lives matter; and indeed for centuries, they have not mattered much. Killing black folk was considered sport, as documented by early twentieth century souvenir postcards where good Christians looked into the camera as that "strange fruit" swung from the trees behind them.[26] The police, with a history to "protect and serve" whites from the menace of blacks, could always kill blacks with impunity. Black lives never mattered in this country, nor do they now—a point made clear as one reads the most recent young black man shot in the back by law enforcers who feared for their lives. It is probably safer for a black man to be in a combat zone in whatever war we are currently engaged than to be stopped by the police in this country. Because black lives matter, I totally support, as an ally in word and deed, this grassroots movement.

Nonetheless, Euroamericans have attempted to create a counternarrative—all lives matter. This disingenuous attempt to diminish the revolutionary cry for justice masks the height of the dominant culture's hypocrisy. If indeed, all lives mattered, then those who benefit from the prevailing social structures would have been at the forefront in dismantling the human rights violations committed against blacks before Trayvon Martin's life was ever threatened for the suspicious act of wearing a hoodie and carrying a box of Skittles, an image that strikes fear, according to then presidential hopeful Hillary Clinton, in the hearts of open-minded white people.[27] The current social, economic, and political structures are undergirded with the recognition that only white lives matter. And while only the idea that white lives matter has been normalized and legitimized, it has become politically correct, under the racist colorblind

26. http://withoutsanctuary.org/main.html.
27. https://www.youtube.com/watch?v=ib_VIGWFufk.

motif, to argue with righteous indignation that all lives matter. Yes, all lives do matter, but the focus is on black lives.

And yet, observing the black lives matter movement, it is obvious that there is an absence of brown lives' participation. Latinx absence is deafening, even as it continues to be ignored. What does it mean to be brown while black lives matter? Care needs to be taken not to fall into the trap of diminishing the importance of the black lives matter movement, as in the case of whites insisting that all lives matter. Still, the continuous black/white dichotomy that has predominately shaped the discourse of U.S. conversations concerning race remains problematic. When President Obama spoke in defense of black lives matter, he said, "I think the reason the organizers used the phrase 'black lives matter' was not because they were suggesting that nobody else's lives matter; rather, what they were suggesting was that there is a specific problem that is happening in the African-American community that is not happening in other communities."[28] Obama's simplistic black/white dichotomy ignores the largest minority group in the U.S. who are also the deadly targets of law enforcement and who, thanks to our immigration laws, now represents the largest population in federal prisons.[29] What African-Americans experience *is* also being experienced in the Latinx community, only the body count is better masked.

How then, do Latinxs stand in solidarity with the black lives matter movement without ignoring that brown lives matter too? While blacks being killed by law enforcement continues to be highlighted in traditional and social media, brown lives barely make the news. Names like Anastasio Hernandez Rojas (age forty-two), a long-time resident

28. Harris, "Obama, in Call for Reform."

29. Moore, "Study Shows Sharp Rise"; Steinhaur, "Bipartisan Push."

of San Diego, remains unknown to the overall American (white and black) conscious. Rojas lived without proper documentation in the U.S. for over two decades. A pool plasterer, he was the father of five children, ranging in age from seven to twenty-three. Attempting to reenter the U.S. after being deported, he was caught and beaten to death by over a dozen Border Patrol agents. Lying facedown with his hands cuffed behind his back, he had his pants pulled down and was repeatedly tasered. An autopsy showed he died of brain damage and a heart attack. Although the beating was captured on a cell phone,[30] one is hard pressed to find any media coverage of this event or any of the twenty-eight killings of other undocumented immigrants by border patrol agents between 2010 and 2014.[31] Also, little is said concerning the five brown undocumented lives that are lost every four days while crossing the desert.[32]

The assassination of Hernandez Rojas is not some isolated incident, but part of a historical norm of brown bodies dying at the hands of vigilante mobs and legal authorities. Although most Americans are cognizant of the historical practice in the South of lynching African Americans, few are aware of a similar normalized and legitimized practice of lynching Latinxs in the West. Mexican Americans were lynched in large numbers throughout the Southwest roughly over the same time when the lynching of African-Americans was rampant in the South. Reasons for Mexican-American lynchings were similar to Black lynchings: acting "uppity," threat of stealing jobs, supposed advances made toward a white woman, cheating while gambling, refusing to leave land coveted by whites, and practicing "witchcraft." Unlike Blacks, Mexicans were also lynched for being "too

30. https://www.youtube.com/watch?v=2y5gpc5Bdbs#t=32.

31. Becker, "Lawmaker Calls for New Investigations."

32. Santos and Zemansky, "Arizona Desert Swallows Migrants."

Mexican," defined as speaking Spanish too loudly, or exhibiting ethnic pride. Mexican women were also lynched for repelling the sexual advances of white men. Like African American lynchings, Mexican lynching occurred with the knowledge and at times with the full participation of law enforcement, specifically the Texas Rangers. Said lynchings became public spectacles conducted in an atmosphere of righteous celebration, and consisted of the victim's body being mutilated with body parts cut off to be preserve as souvenirs. Few, if any whites who participated in these lynchings, both in the South or West, had to stand trial for their actions. And while the number of Mexican lynchings were less than Blacks; nevertheless, it created a reign of terror that helps us understand why brown lives mattered little back then, and today.[33]

Undocumented immigrant lives matter. Documented Latinx lives matter. Brown lives matter. But how do we make this case without taking away from the importance of black lives? And as we claim brown ignored lives matter, we are keenly aware of the other lives of color, and the trans lives that are also being taken. Maybe the real question is why must it be an either/or? According to most demographic studies, whites will represent less than 50 percent of the U.S. population by 2042.[34] In many of our metropolitan cities today, and in several states, whites are already a minority population. This means that in most urban and industrial centers, where communities of color are predominant, the essential American perspective *is* of color. But as U.S. demographics change to the detriment of whites, how is the whiteness of economic, social, and political power fortified? What will a future minority white apartheid America look like? The answer is as old as political maneuvering:

33. Delgado, "Law of the Noose," 298–302.
34. "U.S. Will Have Minority White Sooner."

divide and conquer. As long as communities of color fail to build the necessary coalitions to combat the prevailing reality that all non-white and non-straight lives live in peril, the social structures protecting white privilege will remain intact. Yes, some politically correct cosmetic changes might occur, but over all, the structures that privileges one group over and against other groups will continue unabated.

And while it is easy to simply blame whites for just being whites who, for the most part, ignore what it means to be of color today in America by insisting that all lives matter, communities of color must wrestle with their own complicity. Communities of color are partially at fault for accepting a zero-sum mentality that assumes any advances made by one marginalized group is at the expense of other marginalized communities. Like a four-leaf clover, our separate racially or ethnically distinct cul-de-sacs operate side-by-side with few of us ever venturing into the adjoining community. Solidarity may occur from time to time, but it usually happens with little long-lasting effects. More disturbing is when communities of color are oblivious to how they are locked into structures that cause oppression to other communities of color. How is white racism and ethnic discrimination different from the racist and ethnically insensitive comments emulating from our own communities of color? For example, black leader Al Sharpton once failed to recognize that Puerto Ricans are U.S. citizens.[35] If many of us are content to remain within our own racial or ethnic niche, how can we, then, with any integrity, hold whites to task for not engaging in the liberation of our own community, when we too seldom accompany our neighbors in the adjacent cul-de-sac?

Neither black lives nor brown lives will succeed in the crucial work of dismantling the racist and ethnic

35. https://www.youtube.com/watch?v=XRoa18xxg_U.

discriminative institutionalized structures undergirding law enforcement until brown folk stand in solidarity at Ferguson, and black folk stand in solidarity on the border. Fighting with each other for the crumbs that fall from the master's table only reinforces our subservience and focuses our energies against those who are more our allies than our competitors. Debates as to who has suffered more in this country, blacks or browns, are meaningless. It's not a numbers game, for if just one black or brown life is lost due to institutionalized violence, then that is one life too many, and all our resources must be committed to fight full force to prevent the death of another life, regardless of skin pigmentation. "Black lives matters" must continue. "Brown lives matters" must develop further, of which this book is a contribution to that *lucha*. And just as important, black lives and brown lives must begin a conversation and strategize together for the liberation of all lives from oppressive law enforcement structures that, ironically, see no difference between blacks or browns.

As I spoke to Robert Skiba, I was convinced that for him, brown lives simply do not matter. He fails to see the Latinx—documented or undocumented—as the one who suffers in this immigration discourse. I am convinced that he sincerely believes that it is he, and his fellow white anti-immigrant protestors, who are the ones truly oppressed, the ones facing persecution by their own country. "I resent what the government is doing to the American people," he told me. In his mind, he is the victim. It never ceases to amaze me that those who are most privileged by how society is organized—whose paycheck when compared to women and people of color is substantially higher for doing the same job, who are the first hired and last fired, who disproportionately occupy the largest share of power positions in media, business, and politics—often rewrite themselves into the national narrative as the victims. The creation of the mythology of white men (specifically Christian white men) as victims can be illustrated by an April 13, 2015 broadcast of "Talking Points Commentary of the O'Reilly Factor" on Fox News.[36] Remarking on Hillary Clinton's announcement of seeking the Democratic nomination for the presidency in 2016, Bill O'Reilly said, "If you are a Christian or a white man in the USA, it is open season on you."

By recasting oneself as a victim, whether it is Skiba or O'Reilly, the victimizer is free from having to deal with how societal structure has been normalized and legitimized to privilege them. Individuals like Skiba and O'Reilly refuse to recognize that Euroamericans are the only ones who "belong" in the United States, while others simply live here. When those on society's margins attempt to establish a dialogue to investigate how they too can inhabit this country as full and equal citizens, power-holders whose position within society is jeopardized by such assertions begin to cast themselves as the victims, while labeling those seeking dialogue as "playing the race card" or as "race hustlers." They see themselves under the "tyranny" of those who have historically been oppressed but who now have greater opportunities to advance but, instead, blame whites for all of their problems. White Christians as victims seek the passage of anti-immigration laws disguised as protecting religious liberties, but in fact mask bigotry against those who seek to be accepted as fellow citizens. To declare that it's open season on Christian white men, who continue to hold the reigns on the economic, social, and political power of the nation, becomes coded racist language warning the privileged of the need to advance legislation that suppresses voting rights for people of color, and dismantles

36. http://mediamatters.org/video/2015/04/13/oreilly-hillary -clinton-has-an-advantage-becaus/203271.

pass progressive legislation designed to create a more just and fairer society.

But in one way, O'Reilly is correct. White men like Skiba are, indeed, victims, but not victims in the sense O'Reilly intended. Instead, they are victims of the very structures designed to protect their power and privilege. Because sexism, racism, and ethnic discrimination are interwoven into the very fabric of the history of the United States, everyone, including people of color, is taught their place in society and how they should relate to others. Since childhood, those of us who resided on the underside of history have been taught to see and interpret reality through the eyes of the dominant culture, specifically white, heterosexual, middle-upper class, male patriarchal eyes. In most communities the "white" norm is taught as the legitimate way to interact with others. As this norm is taught, children are forced to suppress their natural inclinations to play and relate with each other at daycare or school. In kindergarten children naturally play together regardless of race or gender, but by the time they reach high school they have been taught and conditioned to sit at different tables in the school cafeteria. They learn to mistrust their fellow students, because they fear being exiled from their own community. "You better not date a Latinx man or I'll disown you," the parent may verbally or, more likely, non-verbally communicate to the child. Or children may learn to remain silent or offer up nervous laughter as the usual response to racist jokes, slurs, or abuses.

Euroamericans, seeing themselves as the norm, are in effect race-less, that is, everyone else is "colored," while they have no color. For example, the dominant culture relatively refers to the black cop, the Latinx teacher, or the Asian mechanic. Seldom do they refer to the white cop, the white teacher, or the white mechanic using "white" as an adjective, mostly because the norm of whiteness makes everyone white unless otherwise stated. Yet, when children reach adulthood, they must begin to deal with the contradictory racial statements, emotions, and mental states that arise with reconciling the need to belong to their group with how they are taught to deal with those of other groups.[37]

The societal structures that cause oppression are not reducible to a formula where only those who are marginalized are the victims. Although it is impossible to equate the suffering of those who are disenfranchised with those who are privileged, it is important to note that those at the center of society are also victims of these structures. They too are indoctrinated to believe they deserve, or earn, or have a right to power and privilege. They are trapped into living up to the false ideal of superiority, and as such, require the same liberation yearned for by the disenfranchised. Liberation is for the abused, from death-dealing social structures that denies them of their humanity, and for their abusers whose own humanity is lost through their complicity with these same structures. Those Christian white men who are not economically privileged, as my PhD mentor John Raines reminded me constantly during my studies, are taught to dream upward, aspiring to become wealthy and to associate with the society's elite, while they blame downward, accusing those who are marginalized of stealing their jobs and depressing wages, thus preventing them from achieving their rightful place in society.

As I leave the anti-immigrant rally of Oracle, I am cognizant that the white protestors truly believe they are fighting for the America of yesteryear, an America that was constructed to protect their power and privilege—in many instances, an unearned power and privilege obtained on the backs of those relegated to their margins. Changing

37. Thandeka, *Learning to be White*, 11–13.

demographics scares them into protecting their place in society by whatever means necessary. Deport the "illegals" becomes the political cry not only of fringe groups at the extreme right, but also the mainstream call of 2016 Republican presidential candidates. Ignored from the rhetoric is the cost of removing 11.2 million undocumented immigrants. According to the American Action Forum, a conservative Republican-based advocacy research group, the price tag will run $400 to $600 billion, will take twenty years to accomplish, and would lead to a $1.6 trillion (or 5.7 percent) drop in the real GDP. These estimates do not include the cost of constructing new courts, prisons, or detention camps.[38]

Demonizing the undocumented, specifically Latinxs, incites them to stand at the ready to stop buses of children. Politicians more concerned with winning elections than becoming statesmen or stateswomen play to the fears of the uninformed to garner votes. Trump proposes to build an impenetrable wall across the border with Mexico paying the cost of construction; Scott Walker sees Trump's wall and raises another wall on the Canadian border; Bobby Jindal claims that immigrants who fail to fully assimilate and learn English are guilty of "invasion"; Chris Christie suggests a tracking system for immigrants a là FedEx packages. And while such fear-mongering has been a staple of the 2016 Republican presidential campaign, states such as Texas have moved to limit the type of ID parents must present to obtain birth certificates of their U.S.-born children, in effect denying birth certificates to many Texas-born children of undocumented immigrants.[39] The 2014 protests of Oracle demonstrate how the demonization of immigrants has contributed to a climate where Latinxs, regardless of

38. American Action Forum.

39. Fernandez, "Immigrants Fight Texas."

documentation, are the ones who really need to fear—fear for their livelihoods, fear for their security, and yes, fear for their safety.

DISCUSSION QUESTIONS

- What purpose does anti-immigrant rhetoric serve? How does blaming the immigrant answer the frustrations of a rapidly shrinking white middle-class? Are immigrants responsible for the loss of white Americans' status? Why or why not? Why do conservative groups, like the Tea Party or those who support the 2016 Trump presidential campaign, find the anti-immigrant rhetoric attractive? Should the undocumented be referred to as "illegals," or "illegal aliens"? Why or why not?

- The undocumented are seen as criminals, tax dodgers, job stealers. Is there any truth to these stereotypes? Why or why not (be sure to provide supportive documentation)? What does it mean to "live on the borders"? Who lives "on the borders"? Where are these borders located? What are the dangers of living "on the borders"?

- What contributions have bananas made to the current immigration crises? What role was played by gunboat diplomacy, the CIA, and United Fruit Company? What moral obligations (if any) does the U.S. have toward Central America—specifically Honduras, Guatemala, and El Salvador?

5

TUCSON'S U.S. DISTRICT COURTHOUSE

THE CLANKING OF SHACKLES, reminiscent of the old chain gangs during the Jim and Jane Crow era, is the first thing I noticed when entering the William D. Browning Special Proceeding Courtroom located in the Evo A. DeConcini United States District Courthouse. The Courthouse is named after a former Arizona Supreme Court justice (1949–53) and the state's former district attorney (1948–49), better known as the father of a former U.S. Senator. Completed in 2000, this fairly new building is located at 405 W. Congress Street, on the edge of Tucson—creating a visual gateway to the desert and mountains that lie beyond.

On a sunny Thursday afternoon, I arrived at this second floor courtroom to bear witness to the injustice of our justice system. Cameras or any other form of electronic recording is strictly prohibited in the courtroom, so I brought a notebook and sat on an uncomfortable wooden bench toward the back-right side of the room. Behind me was a well-dressed man who I later learn was from the Mexican consul dispatched each day to track the defendants' fates. Surrounding me were volunteers from different immigrant rights group, some of which are also here to keep track of the migrants' fate, others to be present in solidarity. Quietly I sat as sixty-four brown men and three brown women, mostly in their teens and twenties, sat silently just a few feet away from me, filling the sixteen seat jury box and an entire set of wooden benches reserved for the public on the left-side of the courtroom. They were manacled individually at the wrist, waist, and ankles. The defendants sat silently in the large courtroom, wearing no belts or shoelaces. Their clothes still contained remnants of the dust from the trails they recently traversed; their bodies unwashed and unkempt, evidence of days of living outdoors, added to the pungent aroma that overwhelmed the courtroom. All needed a good night sleep, a bath, and a shave. They appeared ragged, gaunt, and broken as they sat with blank stares betraying the hopelessness of their situation. Although several seem to be in prayer, crossing themselves before their trials started, our current immigration procedures ensure that not all works for good for those called by God's name.

Photographer: Vincent De La Torre

Throughout their judicial proceedings, I heard the constant clanking of detainees' chains. Chains clanged as they shifted positions in their seats. Chains chinked as they attempted to scratch their nose. Chains clattered as they rose to stand before the bench. This haunting and disturbing sound continued to ring in my ears even as I tried to sleep that evening. Ironically, unlawful presence does not violate federal criminal law. Entering the U.S. without being properly inspected and admitted (illegal entry) is a misdemeanor, which might rise to a felony depending on certain circumstances (8 U.S.C. § 1325). It is important to remember that about 45 percent of undocumented immigrants entered legally but overstayed their visa (as did I). Congress did attempt to make unlawful presence a federal crime (H.R. 4437) in 2005. While the House passed the bill, it failed to be passed by the Senate, due mainly to massive nationwide street demonstrations.[1]

On this day, these sixty-seven brown bodies before me were charged with "illegal entry," a federal petty offense that technically is a lesser charge than a misdemeanor. I asked Heather Williams, then supervisor of the Federal Public Defender Office for the District of Arizona, what would be an equivalent criminal act if committed by a U.S. citizen? After some thought, she responded with "shoving someone on federal land with the intent to shove." Yes—technically they committed a minor infraction akin to a parking ticket, but how many tickets come with the penalty of serving time in a federal penitentiary, or an expulsion designed to permanently separate the accused from their family, friends, and livelihood? Most of us would simply receive a warning, but these individuals must go through this elaborate performance of "justice" so that a very few can profit off their

1. "Modes of Entry."

misery, and the many may sleep in peace under the illusion that our courts of law are just.

The Jesus that is found in our Bibles, and the Jesús sitting but a few feet away from me both undergo a trial before a so-called "impartial" legal system that, in spite of its obvious flaws, contradictions, and biases, is presented as fair. But there is a reason these migrants do not sit in a "court of justice" but instead a "court of law"; we as a society do not seek justice, rather we follow laws. Unfortunately for these sixty-seven brown women and men, laws have historically and consistently been written to the detriment of darker bodies. We are thus left wondering if the purpose of the trial, whether Jesus' or Jesús,' like the purpose of all judicial procedures involving people of color, is to reinforce control over darker bodies by demonstrating what awaits those on the margins of power and privilege who dare to refuse conformity with our current social structures. The punishments meted out by courts of laws are more for the benefit of others from disadvantaged communities to serve as warning, as a deterrent that if they too step out of place, they too can expect similar punishment.

Prior to their trial, they were held at Davis-Monthan Air Force Base, located five miles southeast of downtown Tucson. The base was never intended to function as a prison. Not surprisingly, there were no beds (just benches), forcing most to sleep on concrete floors with only a few receiving blankets. The water fountain did little to quench the thirst of those who recently attempted to cross the sweltering desert, and the lack of cooking facilities at the base offered little in the form of nourishment. If they were carrying any medicine, it was confiscated, placing several (i.e., diabetics) at grave risk, resulting in death for some.

A study conducted by No More Deaths which detailed about 32,075 incidents of abuse and mistreatment of migrants at the hands of law enforcers, reported:

> Individuals suffering severe dehydration are deprived of water; people with life-threatening medical conditions are denied treatment; children and adults are beaten during apprehensions and in custody; family members are separated, their belongings confiscated and not returned; many are crammed into cells and subjected to extreme temperatures, deprived of sleep, and threatened with death by Border Patrol agents.[2]

Based on almost 13,000 interviews with migrants who were in Border Patrol custody, the study discovered that only 20 percent of people in custody for more than two days received one meal. Children were more likely than adults to be denied water or given insufficient water. Many of those denied water by Border Patrol were already suffering from moderate to severe dehydration at the time they were apprehended. Physical abuse was reported by 10 percent of interviewees, including teens and children. The report concludes:

> It is clear that instances of mistreatment and abuse in Border Patrol custody are not aberrational. Rather, they reflect common practice for an agency that is part of the largest federal law enforcement body in the country. Many of them plainly meet the definition of torture under international law. No undocumented immigrant is safe when in the custody of U.S. enforcement agents.[3]

2. No More Deaths, *A Culture of Cruelty*, 4.

3. Ibid., 5.

Jorge, a twenty-seven-year-old Guatemalan, is just one of the 32,075 migrants interviewed. For ten years he lived in Santa Monica, California and, after being deported, was making his way back to his family. Jorge shares a story that unfortunately is not the exception, but the norm. Along with nine other migrants, he was traversing the trails of southern Arizona when Border Patrol agents on motorcycles and horses surrounded them. He was thrown to the ground face first and hit with the butt of a gun while agents hurled insults. For three days he was held at the Tucson processing center where requests to see a doctor for the injuries attained during his arrest were ignored. The food he was carrying (along with $100 U.S. and a birth certificate) were confiscated and never returned. He was only given saltine crackers (which, after days in a desert, would only contribute to dehydration) during his incarceration. The Border Patrol also confiscated their clothes, except for a t-shirt and pants, and then turned on the air conditioning at full blast. Today Jorge suffers from chronic stomach pains resulting from days without eating.[4]

I have spoken to many migrants who have been held by Border Patrol. They provided me with similar testimonies of institutionalized violence. I saw their black eyes, the bruises on their bodies, the fresh scars on their faces. Their testimonies, told to me independent from each other, made collaboration of abuses difficult. Some men, women, *and children*, have experienced psychological abuse in the form of death threats, sensory deprivation or overstimulation, sleep deprivation, and/or the repetitious playing of *migracorridos* (traumatizing morbid songs about dying in the desert) at loud decibels. These forms of psychological abuse constitute torture as defined by the UN Convention Against Torture. Because of a lack of any effective oversight,

4. Ibid., 2.

especially among private prisons that are not required to disclose information in the same manner as government prisons, abuses abound with minimum consequences.

The volume of abuses recounted indicates that we are not speaking of a few rogue agents, but rather, an institutionalized culture of abuse that is widespread and systematic in direct violation of the eighth amendment of the U.S. Constitution that protects the imprisoned from "cruel and unusual punishment." Not surprisingly, the United Nations Human Rights Council released on May 15, 2015 the Universal Periodic Review of the U.S. where more than a hundred international leaders cited hundreds of human rights violations. Although the dominating theme of the report dealt with police brutality towards African-Americans, the report also focused on the excessive use of force and racial profiling of immigrants. Among the 348 recommendations made, the Human Rights Council suggested that each case involving the detention of migrants be carefully investigated to ensure that immigration detention conditions meet international standards. Furthermore, the United Nations assembly opposes the detention of children, a policy embraced by immigration officials.

And yet, in spite of the overwhelming collected testimonies of abuse, the Border Patrol has maintained that no abuses occur. Border Patrol spokesperson for the Tucson Sector, Gustavo Soto, claims that when detainees "leave, they are in 100 percent better condition than when they came in."[5] But there exists no means by which to verify Soto's claims because the Border Patrol has been steadfast in resisting any measure of oversight and accountability. Those who experience abuse are supposed to file a complaint *while still in custody*, ensuring that fear of retaliation would dissuade anyone from stepping forward. Once de-

5. McCombs, "Abuse Tales."

ported, no institutional mechanism exists by which to hold accountable those responsible for abuse.

The accused are brought from the detention center to the courthouse in the morning, even though their arraignment is scheduled for the afternoon. Prior to their hearing, the court-assigned attorney meets with the defendants for the first time, usually in groups, to explain complex legal procedures in a few minutes, procedures that took me (a fluent English speaker with a doctorate) almost half a day to comprehend. Not surprisingly, a study conducted by the University of Arizona showed that 40 percent were simply told by counsel that they needed to sign their deportation and plead guilty; 30 percent of those who signed official documents indicated no one explained the form to them; 29 percent said they had no idea what documents they signed; and 28 percent felt pressure or were forced to sign.[6]

Ten tables are situated before the bench, separated by just a few feet. Each of the ten counselors situates herself or himself at their own table where they confer with clients. Many of the accused use their consultation time to explain why they crossed the border, to explain why they undertook such a harrowing journey, to try to humanize themselves. Children needing food, elderly parents needing medicine, threats of rape or death by ruthless gangs: none of it matters before a judge who refuses to listen to any of these "irrelevant" accounts. The defendants are presented with the government's plea bargain. Most accept the standard plea offered of having a felony charge dismissed if they plead guilty to a misdemeanor and serve a sentence of 30 days to six months. Plead not guilty and face a possible sentence between two to twenty years, depending on one's criminal record. The exploration of possible grounds for asylum or derivative citizenship (having a parental citizen

6. Slack, et al., *In the Shadow,* 23, 29.

connection) was usually skipped or misunderstood during these huddles. Since the consultation occurred in the same courtroom where all the defendants would be convicted—in the presence of court officials, Border Patrol personnel and plain-clothed U.S. marshals—the attorney-client privilege was obviously violated.

On this day, there were ten defense attorneys in the courtroom representing about seven migrants each. For their full day of service (morning consultation beginning at 9 am, and afternoon conviction) they were paid $125 an hour. Tucson pays $3 million a year just to reimburse these attorneys, according to Federal Public Defender Williams. Similar trials as the one I witnessed occur all five days of the week. Hundreds of thousands of the poorest of the poor go through this judicial procedure, a fairly new "zero tolerance" phenomenon known as Operation Streamline—a departure from the previous "catch and release" policy. According to a 2015 report by the U.S. Sentencing Commission, since the implementation of Operation Streamline, "Illegal Re-entry" has become the most commonly filed federal charge, representing 26 percent of all sentencing cases whose offenders are mainly comprised of males (96.8 percent) and Latinx (98.1 percent). Almost everyone convicted for unlawful reentry received a prison sentence.[7]

Prior to 2005, those who entered the country without proper documentation were not prosecuted; they simply were deported through the so-called Voluntary Return process—departure without an order of removal. With a spike in Central American immigrants in the Del Rio, Texas sector who simply could not be returned to Mexico, and civil detention at full capacity, the Border Patrol circumvented the civil immigration system by handing over non-Mexican

7. U.S. Sentencing Commission, *Illegal Reentry Offences*, 1, 27; Light, et al., "Rise of Federal Immigration Crimes," 2.

immigrants for criminal prosecution, a practice, until then, that was limited to those with multiple unauthorized re-entries and/or with a history of violent criminal activities. But in an attempt at "fairness," the U.S. Attorney's Office of the Western District of Texas mandated that all migrants, regardless if they are Central Americans or Mexicans, be criminally prosecuted.

Operation Streamline began December 2005 in Del Rio. By October 2007, Operation Streamline was introduced to Tucson—going fully operational in January 2008. During the height of the program, six sectors participated. As of December 2014, only three sectors continue to participate: Del Rio, Laredo, and Tucson, the busiest being the latter. Originally, deportation triggered a civil sanction barring readmission through legal channels for up to five years. However, by creating an elaborate legal procedure ensuring that before the undocumented migrant is deported, the criminal charge "Entry Without Inspection (EWI)" is added to the civil sanction, the deportee, as a criminal immigrant, is prevented from ever qualifying to enter the country legally.

Magistrate Judge Jacqueline Marshall for the district of Arizona was presiding on this particular day. Session began at 1:30 p.m. sharp. None of the extra counsel tables are removed. As if on a conveyor belt, the shackled defendants are brought before the judge in groups. When asked how they plea on the charge of illegal entry, guilty or not guilty, they each respond *"Culpable,"* Spanish for guilty. On this day, all pleaded guilty, as do 99 percent of all who ever go through Operation Streamline.[8] They were charged, tried, entered a plea, convicted and sentenced in small groups of five to seven. I took out a stopwatch to time how "efficient" justice en masse works. I timed it at one minute and 44.2

8. Lydgate, *Assembly-Line Justice*, 3–4.

seconds or about 20.4 seconds per person, raising grave concerns about due process.

These procedures are a clear violation of the Fifth and Sixth Amendments of the U.S. Constitution because they disregard due process and burden of proof. Specifically, these violations include: 1) appearing before a magistrate more than forty-eight hours after being detained, 2) lack of proof of entry, because they usually are caught within the U.S., not as they are literally crossing the border, and 3) a lack of corroboration of the accused's statement as to entry or alien citizenship.

Operation Streamline is also in violation of the 2009 Ninth Circuit Court of Appeals ruling of *U.S. v Roblero-Solis*, which determined that the taking of en masse pleas violates Federal Rule of Criminal Procedure 11. Additionally, Operation Streamline is in violation of treaties signed with foreign governments. In a report conducted by the U.S. Office of Inspector General:

> [Because] Border Patrol does not have guidance on using Streamline for aliens who express fear of persecution or return to their home countries[;] Border Patrol's practice of referring such aliens to prosecution under Streamline is inconsistent among Border Patrol sectors and may violate U.S. treaty obligations.[9]

And yet, for some, this brand of justice is a game. Take for example Magistrate Judge Bernardo P. Velasco who bragged, "My record is 30 minutes," to describe the speed to trial and conviction of seventy migrants.[10] As I sat in the courtroom that day, I could not help but wonder if what I was witnessing was some type of kangaroo court procedure

---

9. Office of Inspector General, *Streamline*, 2.

10. Santos, "Detainees Sentenced in Seconds."

one would expect to see in an uncivilized nation lacking basic freedoms and human rights, where court proceedings mask injustice but nevertheless serve as an important veneer of legitimacy for the outside world.

About forty of the defendants were charged with a misdemeanor because this was their second attempt to enter the United States. When Operation Streamline first began, more than 70 percent of those prosecuted got "time served." Now, about 67 percent are sentenced to time in prison.[11] Today, everyone received some sentence time, usually longer than a month. Before being hauled off to jail, some of the defense attorneys attempt to provide a reassuring pat on the back or a gentle squeeze of the arm or shoulder, immediately followed by pumping sanitizer from one of the several bottles visible upon the tables before the bench.

To house one undocumented migrant, according to Federal Public Defender Williams, it costs taxpayers $2,000 a month—more than the approximately $850 a year we spend to educate a child in our public schools, thus showing where our treasures truly lie.

Housing all forty convicted on this day would cost $80,000. Realizing that this procedure is repeated each day, taxpayers can expect to spend $1.6 million a month for just the Tucson district. Multiply this by all the federal districts on the U.S.-Mexico border and we are talking about a billion-dollar industry. In Tucson alone, a Warren Institute study calculated the annual cost for a zero-tolerance approach can exceed $1 billion.[12]

An often-overlooked consequence is that crucial law enforcement and monetary resources are diverted from fighting violent crime along the border. In 2002, prior to

11. Trevizo, "Operation Streamline."
12. Ibid.

Operation Streamline, less than 20,000 immigration cases were filed. By 2009, 54 percent of all federal prosecutions in the country, or about 91,899 cases, were for immigration violations. In Arizona, the numbers were higher. In 2010, 84.5 percent were immigration prosecutions, while less than 7 percent were for narcotics.[13] Most of the illicit drugs entering the U.S., according to the Department of Justice, are smuggled through the southern border making the drug cartels responsible for providing supply, the greatest organized crime threat to the U.S.[14] From 2003 till 2009, prosecution of organized crime has dropped by 20 percent, weapons trafficking by 19 percent, and drug trafficking by 20 percent.[15]

Regardless of one's views on immigration, Operation Streamline is problematic because it violates basic human rights, making a mockery of the implied fairness of our judicial system. For those who are concerned about the cost of government, how we process immigrants is definitely not cost effective. Federal Public Defender Williams made it clear to me (and to the Subcommittee of Commercial and Administrative Law when she testified before Congress in 2008), that "Operation Streamline may well be one of the least successful, but most costly and time-consuming ways of discouraging entries and re-entries."

Additionally, it fails to meet its core goal of deterring migrants from crossing the border. The idea was that those caught would serve some time before deportation. Discouraged, they would be deterred from another attempt, telling others they too shouldn't bother due to zero-tolerance. Yet, a study conducted by the University of Arizona revealed

13. Transaction Records Access Clearinghouse, "FY 2009 Federal Prosecutions"; "Arizona Federal Prosecutions."

14. Department of Justice, *National Drug Threat Assessment*, 2–3.

15. Moore, "Push on Immigration Crimes."

that 25 percent of migrants who went through Operation Streamline intended to again cross the border within a week while 56 percent planned to cross again in the future. Deterrence had a minimal impact when compared to factors like family and/or economic needs.[16] Even though the Border Patrol continues to link drops in apprehensions to Operation Streamline, independent researchers and economists argue that any declines are closely related to U.S. economic downturns. The two times since the start of Operation Gatekeeper that the number of undocumented immigrants residing in the U.S. did not increase was during the 2001–2002 and 2007–2008 recessions.

Wherever oppression dwells, there too resides resistance. But how does this resistance form? I argue that the global success of neoliberalism, as demonstrated by CCA and GEO (the two major private prison corporations) makes any hope of liberation from oppressive economic systems unrealistic. The oppressed (i.e., the undocumented) occupy the liminal space between the crucifixion of Friday and the resurrection of Sunday. To occupy Holy Saturday is a hopeless space where all that is known is the brutality and violence of Friday. Sunday remains uncertain, too far away to just wait for. To live in the space of Holy Saturday is to embrace the hopelessness of the moment. To sit in a courtroom awaiting a streamlined trial is to sit in the hopelessness of Saturday. Those with middle-class privilege are usually too much in a rush to get to Sunday. What is needed is to sit with the disenfranchised in the dust (at times the literal dust of the migrant trails), accompanying their suffering. To be hopeless is not to give in to fatalism. The oppressed have no choice but to continue fighting for the basic necessities, regardless of whether they are going to win or not. Only those living with middle-class privilege can

16. Slack, et al., *In the Shadow*, 15.

throw their hands into the air and cry out, "Why bother?" The hopelessness in which the oppressed live propels them toward praxis. Here is the true liberative ethical question: Do we fight for justice because we know we will win, or do we fight for justice, regardless of the outcome, for the sake of justice alone?

What becomes the liberationist response in the face of neoliberalism, which probably will not be vanquished in our or our children's lifetimes? Reflecting on Jesús, with waist, ankles, and wrists shackled at the DeConcini U.S. District Courthouse awaiting trial, has led me to develop an indecent ethics that I call an ethics *para joder* ("an ethics that screws with"). When the oppressive structures cannot be overturned, the only ethical response is to screw with the structures to create disorder and chaos. This is an ethics that employs the trickster image to upset the normative law and order of those in power who require stability to maintain their privileged position.

I had the opportunity to present these concepts to several of the humanitarian groups on the border that work for a more just immigration process. What some immigrant rights activists on the border find useful about this ethics *para joder* is it provides them with new ways of thinking, moving the conversation away from repeating past praxis simply because these are the liberative praxis always done. Reverend John Fife best known for his felony conviction during the 1980s as one of the architects of the Sanctuary Movement (a religious and political campaign that provided safe-haven for Central American refugees fleeing civil conflict in their homeland), is today one of the leading activists of the organization No More Death responsible for providing food, water, and medical attention to the undocumented traversing these trails of terror. Ethics *para joder*, as per Fife "freed us to imagine new possibilities."

I asked him to provide a concrete example. He said that representatives from different immigrant right groups gathered to discuss what they must do next. For decades they have been fighting this battle for justice, and most have lost hope in succeeding. My explanation on how hope can be oppressive leading to discouragement and burnout resonated. Until now, when they tried to think of what to do, they were trapped with having to figure out what dramatic change would look like and then what actions needed to be taken to get to that end goal. When they accepted the hopelessness of the situation, they were emboldened to simply screw with the system, subverting the prevailing oppressive structures. "Screwing with structures of oppression is our calling," said Fife, "We engage in *jodiendo* as we prepare and wait for the movement for justice to take off. Hopelessness frees us to imagine creative ways to struggle for this justice."

On October 11, 2013, around 8 am on a chilly morning, an example of an ethics *para joder* took on flesh. About a dozen activists, wearing bright yellow T-shirts to stand out and adult diapers under their clothes just in case their efforts lasted all day, attempted to halt Operation Streamline. On the Interstate 10 frontage road, they succeeded in stopping two prison transport buses carrying the undocumented to trial that were coming from the short-term detention centers (Golflinks and Swan) on the property of Davis-Monthan Air Force Base and heading toward DeConcini District Courthouse. Once the busses stopped, thanks to a coordinated effort where cars slowed to a stop forcing the busses to do likewise, twelve activists threw themselves under the busses and chained themselves to the front wheels, three per wheel. This was, of course, dangerous for if the bus was not fully stopped and lurched forward, the activist could have been seriously injured, if not crushed under the wheels. As this was unfolding, about a half-dozen other activists chained themselves to the De-Concini Courthouse entrance.

The activists bound themselves to each other using three-foot long PVC pipes with metal bars inside wrapped with chicken wire and a tar substance constructing what the media would call "dragon sleeves." These dragon sleeves covered their linked arms, making it difficult for law enforcers to break them apart. Eventually, with the usage of power tools, the police were able to sever the links and dislodge the protestors. Meanwhile, the protestors succeeded in temporarily shutting down Operation Streamline by laying down their bodies, for five hours, occupying the very space of injustice.

I asked Maryada Vallet, who was chained to the driver's side front wheel of the first bus, why she took such action, literally laying down her body in the streets. After all, she didn't stop Operation Streamline for good and those on the bus got deported anyways. "True," she told me "the seventy on the bus were eventually deported without charges that weekend; nevertheless, we activists participated in the ethical act of *acompañimento*, accompaniment. They accompanied the oppressed while they were in shackles, demonstrating that as the victims of Operation Streamline, they do not stand alone. Even though many of them do attempt resistance, the Streamline system overpowers them, denying the undocumented justice. We accompany them by resisting with them." But weren't these acts of *jodiendo*, screwing with the system too radical? Shouldn't she just start a petition, or write to her Congressperson, or get a permit to protest? Vallet spoke of "moral urgency." She said:

> Lives are quietly being ruin everyday because of Operation Streamline. We must take extremes actions to raise consciousness of this ongoing injustice under the guise of law and order,

> to nudge our community from its complacent slumber. Our actions that day demonstrated an outcry against everyday oppression against immigrant families.

Drawing from Martin Luther King Jr., Vallet explained that petitions and orderly protests are important tactics to build momentum, but it will not turn the tide against powerful systems of injustices.

The activists spent fourteen hours in jail upon arrest, released later that evening on their own recognizance. Originally charged with a felony, the group was found guilty on July 20, 2015 of two misdemeanors (obstruction of a highway and public nuisance) and sentenced to time served, barely a slap on the wrist. When it was Ms. Vallet's turn to stand before Judge Susan Bacal and explain the reason for her participation, she said:

> I locked myself under the Operation Streamline bus as a true expression of my faith. I believe in a God of radical love and inclusion who sets the captives free. Operation Streamline is a modern-day slave trade steeped with racism, selling shackled migrants to fill the beds of private prisons for 30, 60, 180 days, and years if caught again.

It is hopeless to think that a few activist organizations will defeat CCA and GEO along with the many politicians they finance to uphold the prison-industrial complex. But the focus of these activists was no longer on how to shut down Operation Streamline forever, but rather, how to screw with the system and in turn raise consciousness. To that end, they have been successfully *jodiendo* (regardless if they use this term), calling attention and media coverage to an ongoing injustice. I asked Ms. Vallet if she was done with this type of praxis, participating in an ethics of doing as opposed to just contemplating personal piety. Although she expressed gratitude that they were not made into examples and given long sentences; still, the ending was bittersweet. Operation Streamline continues to ruin lives through imprisonment and creating criminal records that would prevent legal migration even if we ever obtain comprehensive immigration reform, thus guaranteeing some families will never be reunited. She sets her eyes to the future, wondering what new actions will be required, recognizing that the bar has been risen. We end our conversation with her telling me, "whatever it takes."

A more recent example of what I'm calling an ethics *para joder* took place on December 14, 2015 when eight clergy members disrupted an Operation Streamline court hearing. As fifty-nine individuals were being sentenced between 30 and 180 days in prison, ministers stood up, one-by-one, and offered prayers or read Scripture, disrupting the so-called "legal" procedures. Among the clergy protesting was John Fife. "I stood in Streamline court today and spoke," he said, "because I have watched too long in silence as Streamline has violated human rights, the Constitution, legal ethics, and my faith. I was called to speak this truth to those responsible, and to bless the poor."

Also disrupting the court procedures that day was Pastor Randy Mayer of Good Shepherd United Church of Christ. "I have attended Operation Streamline more than fifty times over nearly ten years," he says. "Each time I left the court sick to my stomach as I quietly witnessed the abuse of our justice system and the tearing apart of vulnerable migrant families that were only trying to reunite. Today I could no longer be silent. I could no longer allow this 'sham' of justice to happen without my vocal opposition. In this Season of Christmas, we place so much emphasis on family life and we lift up the Holy Family as a symbol of faithful living. As Christmas approaches, I could no longer, with any credibility or integrity, lead my congregation in welcoming the Baby Jesus into our hearts and minds if I sat quietly by as our U.S. Government systematically dismantles and rips apart the very migrant families we honor and celebrate. This matters too much to be silent anymore, and I urge others of faith and conscience to speak out loudly as well."

In a joint written statement explaining their actions, the participating clergy stated: "We have disrupted the courts and we do not do so lightly, for the courtroom is in its own way a sacred place. But we disrupted the proceedings today because they have already been disrupted in a much more troubling way by Operation Streamline. It is clear to us that Operation Streamline is immoral, unjust, and a sin against the poor and their families, and as pastors in this community we have an obligation to speak. And so our witness in the court and in the public square today is: 'You (the shackled migrant workers) are not guilty—this court is guilty of injustice to the migrant poor and their families.' '¡*Tu no eres culpable, este corte es culpable!*'"

DISCUSSION QUESTIONS

- What is Operation Streamline? How did it develop? Is it structurally effective? Cost effective? Is the procedure in line with Constitutional guarantees? Should it be continued? Why or why not?

- What does it mean to live in "Holy Saturday"—to be hopeless because options are not available? How does one seek solidarity with those who suffer and mourn? Is breaking the law permissible?

- What is an ethics *para joder*? Is such an ethics

Christian? What are examples of implementing such an ethical methodology? Is creating chaos ethical? Why or why not?

6

SOUTHSIDE PRESBYTERIAN CHURCH

ALL TOO OFTEN, HOUSES of worship slumber in the light, operating as some sort of country club with a thin veneer of spirituality. The church, or the synagogue, or the temple, or the mosque that ignores the suffering of humanity may be a locale that attracts people of like mind and/or racial and ethnic identity, but it is not a place where the Divine dwells. We live in an era where attendance to houses of worship is declining as their pronouncements fail to register in the national discourse. The quest for orthodoxy, or correct doctrine, has made so many of our faith institutions irrelevant in today's culture and society.

All too often we are more concerned with the treasures found in our offering plates than with the treasures hidden among the outcasts. In fact, faith communities discover their own rich salvation when they commit to orthopraxis, correct action, specifically, the correct action of standing in solidarity with the disenfranchised, the dispossessed, and the disinherited. Only by standing in solidarity with the persecuted does the faith community discover the meaning of justice. Only by sitting at the feet of the marginalized does the faith community discover the purpose for its existence. Only by seeing the face of the oppressed does the faith community perceive the face of God.

All too often, faith communities are more concerned about preaching personal piety then equipping its members to do their faith. In an age of hunger, an age of homelessness, an age of suffering where the elite few are saved through the crucifixion of the many, what faith communities are called to do is preach their faiths not by words but through physical acts of love and mercies toward the least of these. Houses of worship become a light unto a darkened world not by what they believe or by what they preach, but by moving from charity to advocacy to doing justice. The brother of Jesus probably said it best:

> My brothers and sisters, what good is it if someone claims to have faith but does not engage in action? Can such faith save them? Suppose a sister or a bother has no clothes or daily food. If you say to them, "Go in peace; keep warm and well fed," but does nothing about their physical needs, what good is it? Faith by itself, unaccompanied by action, is dead. But someone might say, "You have faith; I take action." Show me your faith without action, and I will show you my faith by my acts. You believe that there is one God. Good for you! But even the demons believe that, and shudder. You fool; do you want evidence that faith without acts is useless? . . . A person is considered just by what they do and not by faith alone. . . As the body without the spirit is dead, so faith without acts is dead (James 2:14–20, 24, 26).

Photographer: Vincent De La Torre

As I sit in the sanctuary of Southside Presbyterian Church, located on the corner of South 10th Avenue and West 23rd Street in Tucson Arizona in the midst of its oldest and poorest Latinx and Native American barrios, I am reminded of the quote that is attributed to St. Francis of Assisi (even though he probably never said it), "I will preach the Gospel at all times, and when necessary, use words." This particular church is neither perfect nor holy; but it is a church that demonstrates its faith by preaching the Gospel all the time without needing to use words. Today, the church provides a shower program where guests can wash and shave, as well as enjoy some food with a cup of coffee. Laundry facilities are provided for guests. Space is provided for day laborers so they can better manage their short-term work opportunities (filling a void after the county's day labor center closed). A legal clinic operates to provide immigration advice to the undocumented. If a tree is indeed known by its fruit, then this church, in spite of all its shortfallings, is a church that believes—not due to its orthodoxy but because of its orthopraxis.

The roots of Southside can be traced to 1870, when President Ulysses S. Grant moved the administration of

Indian reservations from the corrupt Indian Service (currently known as the Bureau of Indian Affairs) to Christian (mainly Protestant) denominations. During his message to Congress that year, President Grant explained that he was "determined to give all the agencies to such religious denominations as had heretofore established missionaries among the Indians, and perhaps to some other denominations who would undertake the work on the same terms— i.e., as missionary work."[1] This policy, known as the Peace Policy, attempted to civilize and Christianize the so-called "savage" by designating a single Christian denomination to be responsible for administering all Indian programs on each reservation, and in return the denomination would hold the monopoly on proselytization. Eighty reservations were divvied up among thirteen Christian denominations. It fell to the Presbyterians to "save" the Papagos (Tohono O'odham).

Towards the start of the twentieth century, Tohono O'odham left the reservation for the city to find employment. Their labor was needed for the railroad and in menial jobs such as housekeeping. Because they were not allowed to live in Tucson, a Tohono O'odham village was established outside the city limits. Being Presbyterians, they attempted to attend the main downtown Presbyterian Church, established in April 1876 as the first Protestant congregation in the city. Confusing the church's comfort for those of the visiting Indians, the congregation thought it best if the Natives worshipped someplace else, ideally outside the city limits, in their own village. So the downtown church raised money for the Indians to have their own building. Southside was founded as a mission church to the Tohono O'odham indigenous people in 1906 on the outskirts of what was then Tucson. The building today is modeled after the Great Kiva of

1. Sherman, "Catholic Mission," 106.

the Anasazi, built using local material (pine logs, flagstone, and saguaro ribs) to reflect the building techniques used for centuries throughout the Southwest. During the 1950s, under the pastorate of Rev. Casper Glenn, the church was engaged in the struggle for racial integration. But what the church is best known for is reviving the religious tradition of sanctuary during the 1980s so as to protect persecuted refugees.

The concept of sanctuary predates biblical times. Those fearing execution or blood-feud retaliation could seek sanctuary at the altar of the local deities on a temporary basis. The church as a place of refuge specifically finds expression in the biblical text (Num 35:6–34) that sets aside six towns within the new so-called Promised Land that were to be given to the Levites (the priestly class) to be sanctuary cities where those who killed someone might flee to avoid the endless cycle of quid pro quo revenge killings or amputations: a life for a life, an eye for an eye. As long as the individual stayed in the sanctuary city, the avenger could not bring him or her (usually him) harm, but if they left the city, they could be killed and the avenger would be held harmless. The purpose of such cities was to provide time and space until the accused could receive a fair trial.

During the 1980s, Central Americans escaping U.S.-sponsored death squads were being denied a fair trial when they migrated to the United States. At that time, Southside responded. They remembered that the faith they were claiming—Christianity—has its bases in the Abrahamic faiths, rooted in stories of refugees and immigrants. The first refugees, Adam and Eve, were cast out of the place they had always known as home. In the stories of the Patriarchs—Abram, Isaac, Jacob, and Joseph—all of them were migrants living at the edge of foreign lands, with Joseph becoming a leading member of the community wherein he settled, contributing to its success. The Exodus narrative and the message of the Prophets remind us to welcome the alien in our midst for we too were once aliens in the land of Egypt. Throughout the New Testament, we are introduced to a God who incarnates Godself as a refugee escaping the persecution of the government of Herod and finding life in exile. An immigration story runs like a thread through the entire biblical text consistently calling us to yoke our faith to the persecution of the alien among us.

Since the fourth century, Roman Law recognized the right of sanctuary—accused criminals could seek protection for a period of time in a sacred place or at a house of worship. This right is based on the regard offered to the sacredness of a locale and the desire of secular officials not to violate sacred space. Under Canon Law, during the Middle Ages, anyone, regardless of guilt or innocence, wealth or poverty, could take shelter at the nearest church and receive a respite from hasty vengeance or legal prosecution. Sanctuary allowed time (usually forty days) for penance and negotiation. By the time of the Reformation, the right of sanctuary was abolished in most countries. But during the 1980s, the right of sanctuary experienced a revival, starting at Southside and spreading to over 567 houses of worship (according to Movement leaders) that openly defied the government and about one thousand congregations, denominations, and associations throughout the U.S. committed to an underground railroad that provided safe haven for Central American refugees escaping violence and death. Seventeen municipalities became sanctuary cities, as did the State of New Mexico, and several colleges and universities. Sanctuary, in our era, has come to be the action taken by a community committed to protecting the basic human rights of those whose rights are being violated by the government, while also being a prophetic witness in holding said government accountable.

During the 1980s, the U.S. foreign policies that established "banana republics" in Central America led to military conflicts in places like El Salvador, Honduras, and Guatemala. Over ten thousand people, including Archbishop Oscar Romero and four churchwomen from the United States, were murdered by the Salvadoran military, a military that the U.S. was funding and supporting. Days before his death, the Archbishop, in an open letter, pleaded with then-President Carter to stop sending military aid to his country because it was only being used to kill its own people. It was common for church leaders and workers to be among those targeted for arrest, torture, rape, and "disappearance" (a euphemism for killing). Graffiti like "Be a patriot, kill a priest," was a common sight among many city walls. Meanwhile in Guatemala, over 50,000 deaths, over 100,000 disappearances, and 626 village massacres took place, the consequences of the CIA involvement in overthrowing the legitimate and democratically elected government of Árbenz.

After taking office in 1980, Ronald Reagan escalated U.S. involvement in Central America, engaging in a geopolitical battle against what he termed "the evil empire." His administration believed that by countering the influence of Cuba and the Soviet Union, human rights would be protected. Throughout the 1980s, almost a million migrants left these U.S.-supported dead zones searching for a safe haven in the United States—usually as refugees. Refugees, according to legal definition, are those who fear persecution due to their race, religion, nationality, political views, and/or their association with political or social organizations. Unfortunately for them, the Reagan Administration refused to grant refugee status, taking the stance that these migrants were simply coming to the U.S. fleeing poverty and not political repression. Those heading North were coming to steal jobs from hardworking Americans. How could they be victims of persecution by U.S. backed governments? The life-or-death fate of these refugees was linked to Reagan's foreign policy objectives. For the Reagan administration, the Central America strategy was to strengthen national security in the fight against global communism.

Central America was understood through the simplistic lens of the Cold War. Any social or political unrest was a result of communist agitators, not legitimate concerns about corrupt military leaders supporting oligarchies that economically and politically oppressed large sectors of the rural population. Refugee status was thus determined by whether the government from where the asylum seekers originated was on good or bad terms with the United States, not by the physical scars or written death threats carried by the would-be asylum seeker. If the U.S. had recognized governmental abuses, then federal law would have barred the Reagan administration from providing any further aid to governments complicit in committing widespread human rights violations. Because Cuba and Sandinista-led Nicaragua had hostile relationships with the U.S. government, those leaving these communist/socialist nations were routinely welcomed with open arms for escaping tyranny, and thus granted refugee status. While 100 percent of all Cubans leaving a non-war zone for the U.S. were granted asylum in 1984, approval rates for Guatemalans and Salvadorans were under three percent.[2]

Because El Salvador and Guatemala were receiving U.S. military aid, these armed conflicts were interpreted as a hot front of the Cold War. Unable to meet U.S. legal requirements for migration as refugees, these applicants, who were usually poor peasants, migrated north without the

2. Gzesh, "Central Americans and Asylum Policy."

necessary documentation, in most cases fleeing for their lives. When caught, they were placed in detention centers until they faced a judge where applicants for political asylum were routinely denied refugee status and deported home to face certain persecution or death. Judges who denied their requests for asylum relied on an opinion letter from Reagan's Department of State that uniformly denied the existence of human rights violations occurring in El Salvador and Guatemala.[3] The irony is that these refugees were fleeing to the country that was supporting the terror in their own country causing the very immigration seen as a threat, only to be deported back to their original countries where they faced torture and death by those trained and financially supported by the same country from which they were expatriated.

Rufina Amaya illustrates the persecution faced by so many of the Central American disenfranchised. Amaya was a poor, middle-aged woman who lived in El Mozote, a small village in El Salvador. On December 11, 1981, government soldiers entered the village and ordered all inhabitants into the streets. Roughly nine hundred civilians, composed mostly of women and children, were shot at point blank. Amaya, who witnessed the event, survived because she was able to hide among some bushes. Recounting her experience, she said, "I heard the screams of the children, and I knew which ones were mine, they were crying, 'Mommy, they're killing us!'"[4] The massacre was conducted by the Atlacatl Battalion, a former Salvadoran Army unit created and trained by the U.S. in 1980 to serve as a counter-insurgent brigade. Ten of the twelve officers responsible for the massacre of El Mozote received their training from the

3. Ibid.

4. *School of Assassins*, a documentary produced by Maryknoll World Productions, 1995.

Western Hemisphere Institute on Security Cooperation (WHISC, formerly known as the School of the Americas) located in Fort Benning, Georgia. WHISC has also trained over sixty thousand Latin American soldiers in commando operations, psychological warfare, and counter-insurgency techniques. In the past, training manuals produced by the Pentagon for WHISC and made public through the Freedom of Information Act advocated executions, torture, false arrest, blackmail, censorship, payment of bounty for murders, and other forms of physical abuse against enemies.

A U.S. Congressional Task Force, headed by former-Representative Joseph Moakley, confirmed that the U.S. Army at Fort Benning had trained those responsible for many of the government-led massacres in Latin America. According to former-Representative Joseph Kennedy, "The Pentagon revealed [through these training manuals] what activists opposed to the school have been alleging for years —that foreign military officers were taught to torture and murder, [in order] to achieve their political objective."[5] Also among the graduates of WHISC were two of the three officers cited for the assassination of Archbishop Romero on March 24, 1980, three of the four officers cited in the rape and murder of the four U.S. church women on December 2, 1980, the founder of El Salvador's death squads and the future president of the country (D'Aubuisson), nineteen of the twenty-six officers cited in the murder of six Jesuit priests, their housekeeper and her teenage daughter at the Central American University in El Salvador on November 16, 1989; and the brutal military dictators that formerly ruled Bolivia, Argentina, Guatemala, Panama, El Salvador, and Honduras, to name a few. Rufina Amaya, the lone survivor of the massacre of El Mozote, concludes, "The only thing

5. Nelson-Pallmeyer, *School of Assassins*, 2–5.

the School of the Americas [WHISC] has accomplished is
the destruction of our countries in Latin America."[6]

In the midst of government-supported terrorism, "a
preferential option for the poor" is what was needed from
faith communities. A liberation theological term first used
in the 1968 Medellín Conference, it signifies God's special
concern for the poor and oppressed and their epistemologi-
cal privilege of better understanding divinity and reality. To
have a preferential option for those who face oppression and
injustice requires that the church actively stand in solidarity
with them in the struggle for a more just social order. On
March 24, 1982, the second anniversary of the assassination
of Archbishop Romero, then senior minister of Southside,
John Fife, declared that the congregation would become a
sanctuary church; thus, making a preferential option for the
poor and oppressed of his time. The congregation voted by
secret ballot to support Fife's declaration, passing with only
two votes in the negative. Although Southside was the first
church to declare sanctuary on January of that same year,
by the time they acted, four other churches (in Los Angeles, Berkeley, Washington DC, and New York City) joined
them. So that there would be no confusion, Fife posted two
banners outside the church building. One read, "This is a
Sanctuary for the Oppressed of Central America," and the
second read, "Immigration: Do Not Profane the Sanctuary of God." On any given night, the church would house
from fifty to one hundred refugees who slept in the church
and/or the Sunday School wing on foam pads. According
to Fife, a modest estimate of over 13,000 refugees sought
sanctuary at Southside.

I asked John Fife where he got the idea of reinstitu-
tionalizing the concept of sanctuary. He recounted a letter

6. *School of Assassins*, a documentary produced by Maryknoll
World Productions, 1995.

he received from a Lutheran pastor from Los Angeles. In the letter, the pastor described an incident concerning a fourteen-year-old undocumented refugee who was running away from pursuing INS agents. In desperation the boy ran into a church and found a hiding place; however, the agents entered the sanctuary, found the boy, and dragged him out. Disturbed by what he witnessed, the Lutheran letter-writer mused what would happen if churches were to revise the Middle Ages concept of sanctuary, of creating time and space until the government could act justly. At first Fife dismissed the letter and concept as impractical, but as time passed, he told me he was left with no other choice but to move in this direction. According to Jim Corbett, a Harvard grad, Quaker, rancher, and cofounder of the Sanctuary Movement:

> We decided to go public because we had all become aware that a full-scale holocaust was going on in Central America, and by keeping the operation clandestine we were doing exactly what the government wanted us to do—keep it hidden, keeping the issue out of the public view.[7]

Cognizant of the tradition of the Underground Railroad that moved African slaves toward freedom in the North, and the failure of European churches who ignored Jews fleeing the Holocaust, church and community leaders chose to lead those dying at the hands of U.S. sponsored Central American death squads toward life. Persecuted Salvadorans and Guatemalans were smuggled across the border and moved to sanctuaries across the country. Because of the work Fife and Corbett were conducting in smuggling and sheltering refugees, the Naturalization Service Agency (INS) sent them a warning in November 1981: cease their

7. Golden and McConnell, *Sanctuary,* 47.

activities or expect to be indicted. They felt they had no choice but to go public with their human rights work, which they did a few months later.

In the mid-1980s, INS decided to follow through on their earlier threats and prosecute the leaders of the Sanctuary Movement, launching a ten-month investigation called "Operation Sojourner." Sixteen sanctuary leaders, including Fife and Corbett, were indicted on seventy-one counts of conspiracy and encouraging, aiding, shielding, harboring, and transporting illegal aliens. The defenders argued they simply were living out their faith, employing the First Amendment free exercise claim. One of the defendants, Sister Darlene Nicgorski, a Roman Catholic nun, stated it best during her arraignment: "If I am guilty, I am guilty of the Gospel."[8]

The defendants argued that they were not breaking the law; rather, it was the Reagan administration that was in violation of the 1980 Refugee Act that aligned U.S. immigration laws with international human rights standards as expressed in the 1951 U.N. Convention and the 1967 Protocol Relating to the Status of Refugees. The 1980 Refugee Act, enacted prior to Reagan taking office, was supposed to create an apolitical process for adjudicating asylum cases on an individual bases employing well-respected humanitarian international standards of determining who is a refugee based on well-founded fears of persecution. But what do you do when it is the government engaged in civil disobedience, of refusing to follow the laws? What is the ethical and moral response when the United States government fails to live up to its international commitments and responsibilities? Foundational to the thinking of the defendants was the Nuremberg Principles of international law. At the close of the Second World War, Nazi generals

8. Curry, "8 of 11 Activists."

and officials were tried for their crimes against humanity. The defense offered was that they simply were following the orders of the State and thus, should not be held culpable for the atrocities committed. The Court found their defense unacceptable, stating, "The essence of the Charter (of the Military Tribunal) is that individuals have international duties that transcend the national obligation of obedience imposed by the individual state."[9]

Justice Robert Jackson (who later became a U.S. Supreme Court Justice) employed the U.S. founding principle that all are "endowed by their Creator with certain unalienable rights." States that violate such rights lack legitimacy. In his opening statement during the Nuremberg proceedings, Justice Jackson said, "The principle of personal liability is a necessary as well as a logical one if International Law is to render real help to the maintenance of peace. An International Law which operates only on states can be enforced only by war because the most practicable method of coercing a state is warfare."[10] International law can only be enforced by war if civil society assumes the responsibility for protecting the victims of human rights violations.

But what happens when the State fails to live up to its commitment to international law? If the State refuses to follow international law and provide basic protections against human rights violations, it falls upon civil society to provide protection to the victims of human rights violation, not as an act of civil disobedience, but as an act of civil "initiative," an ethical concept developed and implemented during the Sanctuary Movement.[11] It would be erroneous to argue that the Sanctuary Movement of the 1980s engaged

9. United States v. Goering, *Judgment of the International Military Tribunal*.

10. Jackson, *Nuremberg Case*, 88.

11. Corbett, *Sanctuary Church*, 17–18.

in civil disobedience as employed during the 1960s Civil Rights Movement. Civil disobedience was a strategy in which Martin Luther King Jr. engaged, because laws based on Jim and Jane Crow prohibited African Americans from participating as full citizens. Unjust laws were purposely and publicly violated in order to raise society's consciousness. Employing civil disobedience proved successful as legislation designed to provide equal access and protection were introduced and passed. Obviously, inequality persists; but the issue is no longer bad laws, rather how the good laws are ignored. The goal of the Sanctuary Movement was not to change bad laws, because U.S. refugee laws were good laws in that they conformed to international standards. The problem was that the U.S. government was violating its own refugee laws by refusing to recognize those fleeing persecution in Latin America; hence, if anyone was engaged in civil disobedience, it was the U.S. for refusing to follow international standards.

Jim Corbett, one of the defendants, coined "civil initiative" to "correct the maladministration of an existing body of laws." Those practicing civil initiative are called to: 1) neither evade nor seize police powers, but stand ready to be arrested, and if they are, demand a trial by jury; 2) be truthful, open and subject to public examination; 3) strive toward being catholic, protecting the rights of the abused regardless of their ideology or their political usefulness; 4) seek to be dialogical, treating government officials as persons, not simply adversaries, in the hope of reaching a reconciliation that does not compromise human rights; 5) remain germane to the needs of the oppressed to be protected and not simply focus on media attention; 6) be a volunteer-based operated; and 7) community-centered.[12] Based on the logic that condemned Nazi officials, civil ini-

12. Ibid., 19, 23–24

tiative is a praxis based on the existing moral obligation to render succor to victims of human rights violations; recognizing international duties transcend individual obligations to obey national states.

In preparation for the Tucson Sanctuary trial, the government paid informants with seedy backgrounds to infiltrate the churches to engage in the same supposed "illegal" activities that the defendants were being accused of. Ironically, there was no need for informants because all the defendants were quite transparent about what they were doing, even to the point of flaunting their activities. Fife, in a letter, took the extraordinary step of placing the U.S. Attorney General on notice concerning the actions in which his church engaged.

During the trail, the defendants were denied basic constitutional guarantees of preparing and presenting available legal defenses and the right to testify on their own behalf. Prosecutors filed a motion in limine, a motion protecting the procedures from any prejudicial questions or statements. In other words, the defendants were prohibited from mentioning 1) international law, 2) the Refugee Act of 1980, 3) their religious faith or convictions, 4) U.S. foreign policies in Central America, 5) current events in Guatemala and El Salvador, and 6) the testimonies of persecuted refugees. The only thing the defendants could address was if they harbored and transported undocumented migrants. In affect, the Tucson Sanctuary trial was more akin to a "political show trial" one would expect from totalitarian governments like those which occurred under Stalin, the apartheid trials that convicted Mandela, or the Castro trials against counterrevolutionaries, where a veneer of legitimation was maintained. The motives and conduct of the trial was based more on political motivation than the rule of law.

The defendants went on the offensive and filed a civil suit against the Attorney General for U.S. violations of refugee laws. After three years of legal maneuvering the U.S. government settled the case, agreeing to provide temporary protective status to the refugees, ended all deportations of Guatemalans and Salvadorans, and instituting reforms on how to conduct asylum requests. Nevertheless, all the defendants were found guilty and sentenced to five years of probation. When asked if he would continue to help transport and house refugees from El Salvador and Guatemala, Fife responded, "I plan, for as long as possible, to be part of a congregation that has committed itself to providing sanctuary for refugees."[13] The government may have "won" the legal battle by obtaining convictions of the defendants, but by 1990, they lost the war. Leaders of the movement take great pride that not one person who sought sanctuary at one of their houses of worship was deported.

By the early 1990s, the need for sanctuary came to an end; but this was also when NAFTA was being debated, ratified, and implemented. This was the time when Operation Gatekeeper was being executed, a wall was being built, and a border was being militarized. "Bottom line in all these activities," says Fife, "is the government's failure to observe human rights standards and the lives of literally thousands of poor, desperate people, whose lives are on the line because government policy that ignores refugee rights, human rights, basic human rights." So the work of the Sanctuary Movement leaders continued, but with a new mission to save lives, only this time, lives were being lost on the border as a direct result of our immigration policies. They began with setting water in the desert and remote places where migrants traverse. They organized and created organizations like Humane Borders, Samaritan Patrol, and No More Deaths.

13. Curry, "8 of 11 Activists Guilty."

Death in the desert is used as official policy by the U.S. government to serve as a deterrent for other migrants trying to cross—a gross violation of basic human rights. Rather than offering sanctuary to these migrants as they did in the 1980s, effort first went into immigration reform, changing policy through the political process. But over twenty years have passed since NAFTA and people with brown skin continue to be offered up as living sacrifices so that those with the privilege of living within the U.S. borders can have a materially abundant life. "It's not enough to write a letter to your Congressional representative, it's not enough to picket in front of a federal building, especially when the lives of people are hanging in the balance," says Fife, "We *have* done all that, but it is not enough."

In light of the failure of finding a political solution, several churches, starting with Southside, began to call for a New Sanctuary Movement. I spoke with the current pastor of the church, Alison Harrington. "The place of hopelessness," she tells me, "is where solidarity begins, where we commit to do the hard work." The hard work that Harrington is referring to is the saving of lives from injustices. On August 7, 2014, Rosa Imelda Robles Loreto, a forty-one-year-old house cleaner and mother of two, entered Southside and requested sanctuary. Robles Loreto owns a house, pays her taxes, and has no criminal record. Robles Loreto recounts her testimony: "I have been living here for sixteen years, and my work has always been housecleaning. I've only been stopped once. On my way to work in September 2010, I was stopped by a sheriff for a minor traffic violation. Instead of giving me a ticket, he called for immigration authorities and I was sent to detention." Fearing separation from her children, Robles Loreto sought sanctuary. "When I entered in sanctuary," she says, "we thought it would be days, a month, before my case would be closed. But then came forty days. Then a hundred. Then we celebrated Christmas in the church, and my children's birthdays. I missed the first all-star tournament of my son José Emiliano, nine years old. My older son, Gerardo, twelve years old, went to Washington to intercede on my behalf. We celebrated my birthday here in July, and now my children have returned to school."

Twenty-three days before Robles Loreto sought sanctuary, Pope Francis called for a change in the way migrants are viewed. The Roman Pontiff stated, "Many people forced to emigrate, suffer, and often, die tragically; many of their rights are violated, they are obliged to separate from their families and, unfortunately, continue to be the subject of racist and xenophobic attitudes."[14] Robles Loreto is just one among millions who is subject to racist and xenophobic attitudes. So why does Robles Loreto get sanctuary? "Sanctuary is not about going out into the community to find the person to be the poster child of the movement," Harrington tells me, "Its about who shows up, knocking at your door, looking for help. While Rosa is a leader in this movement, she didn't need to fit into the mythical 'good migrant' archetype—she's a mom who loves her kids, and that's enough for us." The church, along with the movement, does not decide whom to assist based on who is worthy or not worthy, who is exceptional. Instead, they recognize their calling to struggle against injustice.

"People are snatched up in the middle of the night, on their way to work," says Harrington. "They disappear and get lost in the labyrinth of our immigration system. We are called to take care of the orphans and widows, yet our immigration policies are making orphans and widows of the families being left behind." Robles Loreto asked for sanctuary because she does not want to make her children

14. Harris, "Pope Denounces 'Racist, Xenophobic'".

orphans and her husband a widower. Her husband Gerardo Grijalva provides landscaping services in the Tucson area and is also facing the threat of deportation; her children are in school. The children come regularly to the church where they play catch and baseball as their mother looks on. "At least," their mother says, "I get to see my boys play."

"It would be easy for us who face deportation orders to change our name or address to stay here with our families," says Robles Loreto. "But sanctuary gives an option to demonstrate to the government and ICE that we can take the right course. We have always followed the rules in the U.S., and we want to show that we will keep fighting for an opportunity and not hide from our responsibilities." Robles Loreto was welcomed by Southside without being asked her religion, or if she belonged to any church. She was an alien in our midst, and the church took her in. I asked her why she sought sanctuary. "I know people are looking at me," she responded, "I'm not only fighting just for my family, but I am fighting for the thousands of other mothers that are in my same situation." She spends most of her time in a twelve-by-twelve room that was once the pastor's office. It is a cramped room with bunk beds, a television that she watches most of the time out of boredom, and assorted chairs for friends and family to sit. A portrait of her family hangs on the wall, a constant reminder of how close and far she is from them. Most evenings she just surfs the internet. About a dozen individuals nationwide find themselves in a similar predicament, seeking sanctuary in a house of worship. This self-imposed prison, she tells me, this last result might provide hope for others living in the shadows. "We want to move from the shadows," she says, "We are tired of hiding, we want to live in the open. But don't separate us from our families, don't separate a mother from her child."

Not only is Robles Loreto saved by the actions of the church, so too is the church saved by the presence of Robles Loreto. In response to Europe's 2015 Syrian refugee migration, Pope Francis challenged a crowd in St. Peter's Square after reciting the traditional noon Angelus prayer, to make migration a major social cause of the church. "May every parish, every religious community, every monastery, every sanctuary in Europe host a family," said the Pontiff.[15] Muslims housed in Christian churches places the focus on the trials and tribulations of the immigrant, and not their religious faith (or lack thereof), nor their nationality, nor their political views. The focus is on the injustice faced that causes immigration. For individual houses of worship to take in one family personalizes the crisis, moving it from some abstract number of people seeking refuge to the injustices being faced by one person with whom church members house and share a meal. Imagine if houses of worship were to take up the Pope's challenge here in the U.S. when dealing with our own migrants.

Immigration reform would come about quicker if the churches were to open their doors to the one gently knocking asking to be let in. "In the face of the tragedy of tens of thousands of refugees fleeing death in war or hunger, and who are on the road to hope of life," the Pope continues, "the Gospel calls us, asks us to be near, the littlest and the abandoned." Leading by example, the Vatican has offered sanctuary to several families.[16] For Pope Francis, the church should globally open its doors to everyone, without exception. At times, he says, the church keeps Jesus "prisoner" in its own institutions and does not let him out into the world. "The house of God is a refuge, not a prison!" the Pope cried

15. Rocca, "Pope Francis Calls On."
16. Ibid.

out. "And if the door is closed, we say: 'Lord, open the door!' Jesus is the door that lets us enter and exit."[17]

"I always ask myself," says Robles Loreto, "what it would be like if the American people and I had the opportunity to come to know each other. People would realize that my family is equal to theirs. We are mothers and fathers who would give their lives for their children to fulfill their dreams. We are equals, and just because an immigrant made a mistake does not mean we all should be judged the same. And those who carry hatred against us would see that we are all brothers and sisters, children under the same God." For 461 nights Robles Loreto slept at Southside, cooking her meals in the church's kitchen. On November 10, 2015, about two hundred people gathered at Southside to bid Robles Loreto farewell and watch her take her first steps toward freedom after an agreement was reached ensuring her to leave the sanctuary safely.

John Fife provides us with four enduring lessons that faith communities can learn from the Sanctuary Movement:

> First, that the church can be an effective community base for active, nonviolent resistance to government violations of human rights. Second, the church has a responsibility, both legally and morally, to protect the victims of human rights violations. We called it civil initiative: the legal right and ethical responsibility to protect the victim of human rights violations when government is the violator. . . . Third, the church is a global institution capable of forming effective relationships to protect the poor and persecuted across national borders. Fourth, by entering into protective community with the poor, the church becomes spiritually transformed. . .[18]

17. McElwee, "Francis Cries Out."

18. Fife, "New Sanctuary Movement."

"Every church," Pastor Harrington informs me, "should determine for itself how to be a disciple of Christ in the midst of scary injustices. What is our call, not just how do we prop up the institutionalized church so it can survive?" In a small courtyard at Southside there is a pile of stones with names written on them and dates. Every year, the church conducts a migrant Sunday service. The names of those who perished crossing the border over the past year are written upon these rocks. The word "*desconocido*," unknown, appears on many of these stones. I have been visiting this church for over a decade now. I am deeply grieved at how high the pile of stones has gotten.

DISCUSSION QUESTIONS

- What does it mean that the church is "asleep in the light"? What responsibilities, if any, does the church have toward the undocumented? What specifics acts should a church engage? Does a dichotomy exist between faith and social action? Why or why not?

- What is sanctuary? What are its religious/historical roots? What role did it play in contemporary U.S. history? What is the School of the Americas and what role did/does it play? Is the ancient religious ritual of sanctuary relevant for current times? Why or why not? What does it mean to enter sanctuary today?

- What is civil initiative? How did the concept develop? How does it differ from civil disobedience? What role did it play in the Sanctuary Movement? What role does it play in today's ethical analysis?

7

BACK TO NOGALES, MEXICO

WE SAY OUR IMMIGRATION system is broken, but seldom
do we contemplate how our immigration system is breaking lives. Many preach family values while ignoring how
their desire for cheap goods are subsidized by breaking
apart Latinx families. Simply stated, brown families don't
matter. Sandra Lopez is just one life being crushed under the immigration-grinding mill. I sat with Ms. Lopez,
twenty-two years old, for several hours to hear her story,
just a month after she was released from prison. My impression of this young woman, who spoke with a deep sense
of maturity and confidence, was that any organization, for
profit or non-profit, would be lucky to have her working for
or representing them. She spoke with purpose, determination, and a wisdom that surpassed her young age. On the
side of her palm was a tattoo with just one word "Faith," an
indication of a life that had little options but to rely on some
blessed assurance.

Photographer: Vincent De La Torre

She came to this country when she was less than a month old. Her mother married an American and began to create a new home in Tucson for her daughter. Sandra flourished in school, excelling in her studies and graduated from Amphitheater High School as an honor student. Barely speaking Spanish, Sandra was a typical American teenager until she wanted to attend Pima Community College. Lacking a social security card meant she would not be able to achieve her dream of studying medical science. Instead, at nineteen, she took a menial job at a local meat market. "Honestly, my dreams crashed," she told me, "I was unable to continue my studies, I was forced to live in the shadows. I felt my life was over for me." She lived a precarious life, always at risk of being torn away from her family and friends. Like so many Latinxs, Ms. Sandra belongs to a mixed status family where she, her mother and older sister are undocumented while her two young siblings are U.S. citizens.

On September 1, 2010, a friend asked her to mail a package for him. "I made a big mistake," she tells me, "I trusted a friend that I shouldn't have trusted." He was late to work and just needed a Good Samaritan to drop a package at the post office for him. Sandra agreed, going to the local Fed Ex store. Paying the postage with the $100 her friend gave her she received $14.59 in change that she got to keep for her troubles. After mailing the package, she went on her way. Upon leaving the shop she was stopped and arrested because in the package, unbeknownst to her, were 3.4 pounds of marijuana. Charged with a class three felony (possession of marijuana for sale) she plea-bargained to a guilty plea of "securing the proceeds of an offense" ($14.59) on February 8, 2011, sentenced for time served and placed on three years probation. For most young persons, this slap on the wrist would have served as a cautionary tale not to be so trusting of so-called friends, a lesson that could have contributed to her becoming a productive law-abiding citizen. But Ms. Lopez was undocumented, and this minor lapse of judgment meant life-altering consequences, starting with a transfer to ICE and placed at Eloy Detention Center, a 1,500-bed facility owned and operated by the private prison industry, Corrections Corporation of America (CCA).

Creating a judicial procedure that criminally prosecuted violators of immigration policies has been a boon for the private prison industry. Leveling criminal charges is highly profitable. Once sentenced, defendants are handed over to the Federal Bureau of Prisons who in turn places these undocumented immigrants in for-profit prisons, which in 2015 represented 62 percent of all immigration detention beds.[1] The for-profit prisons are mainly operated by the CCA, which controls 92,500 beds in sixty-seven facilities;[2] and the GEO Group, which controls 73,500 beds

1. Shah, et al., *Banking on Detention*, 1.
2. CCA 2012 Annual Report.

in sixty-six facilities.[3] Together, these two corporations represent the vast majority of the private prison market.

Ironically, during the 1990s, CCA was on the verge of bankruptcy and GEO stock were at an all-time low. Fortunately for them, during the first decade of Operation Streamline (2005–15), the detention system increased by 75 percent.[4] Unprecedented rates of undocumented border-crossers were, and continue to be, incarcerated on average for 180 days; overburdening the federal criminal justice system, but providing tremendous revenues to the for-profit private prison industry. The incarceration cost to the American taxpayer since the start of Operation Streamline through 2012 has been $5.5 billion, with much of this money going directly to CCA and GEO.[5] In 2012, the federal government used taxpayers' money to compensate CCA $757 million (plus $1 billion in state funds) and GEO $533 million (plus $947 million in state funds) for contracted services.[6] While these corporation charge the U.S. government about $164 a day to house one immigrant, community-based alternatives can provide the same service at about $12 per day.[7] And while the so-called "common wisdom" is that private prisons are more efficient and cheaper than state-run prisons, a study conducted by the Arizona Department of Correction revealed that state-run prisons could cost $1600 less per inmate per year. The study also showed how the illusion of more cost-effective private prisons was maintained by their refusal to accept relatively

3. GEO Report (http://perma.cc/PC9A-7KY4)

4. Shah, et al., *Banking on Detention*, 1.

5. Robertson, et al., *Operation Streamline*, 3.

6. Tartaglia, "Private Prisons, Private Records," 1695–96.

7. Detention Watch Network, *About the U.S. Detention and Deportation System.*

unhealthy prisoners, leaving their higher maintenance to the state and the taxpayers.[8]

To ensure the profits of these for-profit prison, almost two-thirds of all prison contracts mandate a minimum occupancy level (usually 90 percent), and if the government is unable to supply sufficient inmates to meet the minimum occupancy, then taxpayers must pay for empty beds; hence an incentive to send more migrants to prison. Furthermore, Congress mandates that at least 34,000 immigrants must be detained on any given day. Corporate profits and political donations are exchanged for the imprisonment of brown bodies. No wonder these for-profit corporations, since 1989, funneled more than $10 million to political candidates (with Republicans being the main beneficiaries) and have spent almost $25 million on lobbying efforts for legislation like Arizona's highly controversial anti-immigrant laws.[9] These lobbying efforts ensure the writing of state and federal laws that requires imprisonment for the undocumented. This broken system can never be fixed, for if it ever were, these for-profit prisons would lose billions in federal monies and possibly go bankrupt.

Private for-profit prisons are not much better then Border Patrol detention centers. A few inmates in these private corporations have died while in detention for not having access to their medications—a clear violation of the eighth amendment of the U.S. Constitution and the Geneva Convention. Others died under suspicious circumstances. Take for example the May 20, 2015 death of 31 year-old Jose de Jesús Deniz-Sahagun at Eloy Detention Center. Deniz-Sahagun was allegedly beaten by guards before he was placed in isolated confinement. U.S. Immigration and Custom Enforcement (ICE) issued a press release that

8. Oppel, Jr, "Private Prisons Found to Offer Little."
9. Cohen, "How For-Profit Prisons."

contradicts the detainees' charges, claiming Deniz-Sahagun died of "unknown causes after being found unresponsive by facility personnel."[10] A subsequent autopsy revealed he died of asphyxiation; a sock was found lodged in his throat. According to CCA, who operates Eloy Detention Center, at least thirty-two detainees, including seven suicides, died at their facility since 2004.

On June 13, 2015, two hundred men launched a weekend hunger strike when they sat down in the recreation yard of the detention center at 9:45 am. They were responding to what they claim are guard beatings, inhumane conditions, and the systematic abuse of power responsible for Deniz-Sahagun's death. Those striking also called for an end to the exploitation of their labor. Detainees who are refused work in the U.S. are forced to work at corporate detention facility for $1 a day. They are demanding an independent investigation into recent deaths, some which have gone unreported. ICE, however, claims that no detainee has gone on a hunger strike, even though they do recognize the protest. And while undocumented federal prisoners have been killed while incarcerated at the hands of prison guards, as in the case of Deniz-Sahagun, others died through the denial of lifesaving medicine, as in the case of Edimar Alves Araujo. Picked up in 2007 for a traffic violation, Araujo was turned over to ICE when it was discovered he lacked proper documentation. While in custody at the Woonsocket Rhode Island detention facility he suffered an epileptic seizure. His sister Irene rushed to the facilities with his daily medication, but officers refused to provide Araujo with the needed medicine, leading to his death.[11] Araujo's experience is

---

10. ICE Newsroom, "ICE Detainee Passes Away."

11. Fears, "3 Jailed Immigrants Die."

common, as 37 percent of those who requested medical attention while incarcerated reported receiving none.[12]

Latinxs, who represent about 18 percent of the population, now comprise the majority of all people in federal prison, thanks to Operation Streamline. Of course, not every migrant caught crossing the border experiences this legal procedure. An undocumented number are simply deported without any trial, raising concerns of number manipulation to demonstrate fewer convictions (hence incorrectly associating these numbers with fewer immigrants crossing as argued by Homeland Security), which falsely justifies that militarizing the border since 1994 is indeed working. And yet, while claiming success, more prisons are being built. The amount of profits to be made has these corporations building detention centers that can now house the whole family—mothers and children. In December 2014, a for-profit detention facility was opened in Dilley, Texas with the capacity of housing 2,400 mothers *and their children*. We are a nation that has infants and children behind bars! When seven House members visited the Dilley facilities, they were met with chants in Spanish of "We want freedom!" At first, the situation appeared to be changing. On June 24, 2015, Homeland Security announced plans to end long-term detention of mothers and children caught crossing the border once they pass the first hurdle of the asylum process, an interview to voice their fears for returning home. However, by August 2015 the Obama administration, while agreeing with the June reforms, nonetheless argued that facilities housing mothers and children remain an effective tool in deterring border crossings.[13]

On March 9, 2011, a month after being transferred to Eloy Detention Center, Ms. Lopez appeared before a

12. The Center for Latin American Studies, *In the Shadow*, 24.

13. Laughland, "Justice Department Asks Judge."

magistrate who asked if any of her parents were American citizens. Assuming he meant biological parents, she responded no. Did she have any children who were U.S. citizens or was she married to a U.S. citizen? Again, the response was no. The judge told her that she therefore had no relief. Crying, distraught, and scared, she was asked to sign a Voluntary Repatriation Order (which she did not understand) authorizing her deportation. Sadly, if she instead would have said that her stepfather was a U.S. citizen, she would not have been deported and her nightmare could have been averted. Due to her misunderstanding of the judge's questions and unaware of her rights, within a few hours, she was deported to Mexico. She would have been eligible for the Deferred Action for Childhood Arrivals (DACA) that allowed those brought to the U.S. as young children (under the age of sixteen) to apply for work and school and be protected from deportation for at least two years. Unfortunately this new policy wasn't enacted until June 15, 2012.

Ms. Lopez was deported on the same day of her court hearing, with limited Spanish skills and knowing no one to a country she had never visited. On the ride to the border, many of the persons on the bus were transnational migrants. Three out of four U.S. agricultural workers are Mexican born, and a growing representation in manufacturing, construction, and the service sector. During the 1990s, when NAFTA was implemented, the flow of migrants to the United States was ten times higher than the previous two decades. About ten million people who were born in Mexico now reside in the United States constituting, along with U.S. citizens of Mexican descent, the world's largest diaspora located in one country. The remittances, or "migradollars" send home (destined mainly for household consumption) represents the second-largest source of foreign exchange Mexican earnings, greater than either tourism or agricultural exports. Some of these migrants made the torturous journey north to earn enough to build their own house or buy a truck when they return. Others left to provide ongoing financial support for families left behind, including teens who face familial pressure to leave school and head north to contribute to the survival of the family.[14]

Criminalized in the United States, these migrants are the true economic heroes of Mexico. In the absence of any real federal Mexican development projects, migrants "are held accountable for promoting progress in a situation where the state, claiming minimal interference, declines to take responsibility."[15] The people on the bus, the poorest of the poor who are despised in the U.S. in spite of their desire to work, are probably the greatest contributors to the reduction of Mexican rural poverty. And yet, the contributions made for the sake of the family is tearing those same families apart as husbands who leave wives and children behind abandon them after some time. Kids growing up without dads simply plan to head north and thus abandon school and other familial responsibilities.

When Ms. Lopez arrived at the border, she was taken off the bus and told to go with no identification. Thirty-nine percent of those interviewed for a University of Arizona study reported that their possessions, cell phones, clothing, food, and most important, identification papers, were confiscated and not returned when deported. Millions of dollars, thousands of cell phones, and thousands of identification papers are simply taken. Many lose irreplaceable birth certificates or other important identification papers.

14. Fitting, *Struggle for Maize*, 179, 185.

15. Delgado Wise and Márquez Covarrubias, "Capitalist Restructuring," 1372.

To be deported with nothing is to be made terribly vulnerable, exposed to the weather, and worse, to criminal exploitation, with no means of contacting love ones or friends for assistance. Mexicans lacking proper identification reported frequent harassment by Mexican authorities that accused them of being Central Americans. Lack of identification also makes it difficult for them to obtain temporary employment to raise funds for a bus ticket back to their hometown. They cannot even call home to have family members wire them funds because an ID is required to pick up wired money.[16] Unable to afford food or a means of returning to their hometown, they have little choice but to attempt another border crossing, only this time, if they die during the trek, they could easily remain unidentified.

Ms. Lopez was but one of the 600,000 to 800,000 undocumented migrants deported each year.[17] Like so many vulnerable women, she was deported to a dangerous border town after all the social service aid offices were closed. Deporting a young teenage woman into potentially dangerous conditions is the established norm maintained in the name of deterrence, making the situation so life threatening that it would supposedly deter others from migrating into the United States. During the first six months of 2008, 18,249 children under the age of eighteen were repatriated. Of those, we literally dumped around 10,000 children, without any adult supervision, on the Mexican border. And to make matters worse, many (mostly single women and children) are sent across the border after dark where they become easy prey for criminals.[18] It is common to repatriate women and children to unfamiliar cities at night after shelters and other services are unavailable, in violation of Article 3c & f

16. Slack, et al., *In the Shadow*, 24.
17. Kino Border Initiative Annual Report 2014.
18. "Mexicans Deported from U.S."

of the February 20, 2004 Memorandum of Understanding signed between the U.S. and Mexican governments.

Ms. Lopez arrived in Nogales, Sonora with about $30 in her pocket. In some ways, she was "lucky." Border Patrol routinely engages in lateral repatriation as part of its deterrence strategy, sending repatriated immigrants to unfamiliar border ports miles away from their original point of entry, at other times they engage in remote repatriation sending Mexican nationals to the interior of their country.[19] To create greater hardships, families are split up and denied information concerning the whereabouts of their relatives. They are held in custody separately and repatriated through different ports of entry on different days making it difficult, if not impossible for them to reunite, also a violation of Article 3e of the 2004 Memorandum of Understanding signed between the U.S. and Mexican governments. Guadalupe and Marco Antonio from Guadalajara experienced such a fate, when the wife was deported to Nogales while the husband was repatriated to Mexicali, over 400 miles away, or a nine-hour drive. Efrain, another deportee, was separated from his sixteen-year-old sister. When Efrain was deported, he had no information about his sister, if she was already deported, and if so, to where.[20]

Ms. Lopez at least had $30. Arrested migrants have their cash confiscated and receive a debit card or a check that they are unable to cash outside the United States. Few ever received their possessions back, as the wealthiest nation ever known to humanity literally takes the clothes off their backs, stealing the meager possessions of the world's dispossessed. Once off the bus, some women offered

19. Light, et al., "Rise of Federal Immigration Crimes"; No More Deaths, *A Culture of Cruelty*, 8.

20. No More Deaths, *Crossing the Line*, 19; No More Deaths, *A Culture of Cruelty*, 23.

assistance. "*Mija*, we will help you survive and get back across the border," they promised. "Many young girls do this to survive, come with us, food and shelter is what is most important now. All you have to do is prostitute yourself." She approached a police officer to ask directions to the local humanitarian aid station, but all humanitarian centers were closed. Instead, the officer offered to buy her a meal suggesting sexual favors in exchange for his protection.

One of the humanitarian aid centers that could have helped Ms. Lopez if she was deported during the day as opposed to after-hours is the Kino Border Initiative (*Iniciativa Kino para la Frontera*). Started in 2008, the center is located five minutes walk from the Nogales-Mariposa Arizona Port of Entry in a small, modest concrete building. It provides direct aid, specifically meals for fifteen days to those repatriated. When I visited the center, I noticed the long line of hungry deportees that formed early. They looked tired, exhausted, defeated, and despondent. Several had difficulty walking due to sprained ankles and blistered feet obtained while attempting to cross the border. Others showed me black and blue marks that they claimed were caused by the physical abuse endured while in detention at the hands of border agents. Those recently arrived have no money, no phone, and just one set of clothing, which they are wearing. All are holding a receipt dated by Mexican border authorities indicating when they were repatriated. Before entering *el comedor*, they must show the precious deportation document to the volunteer at the door to obtain passage.

Along the walls are posters with uplifting messages like, "All people have the same rights," or "I have the right to live a life free of violence" written above a white dove with an olive branch in its beak. On one wall is a subversive mural, a version of "The Last Supper," with male and female migrants as the apostles eat with Jesús, who is wearing a backward baseball cap. In 2014, Kino served 38,677 meals, housed 517 women and children, and treated 2,034 migrants for injuries and illnesses.[21] As mentioned earlier, Mexican banks often reject the U.S. checks or debit cards given to migrants in exchange for the cash confiscated by Border authorities. At times, a volunteer at Kino's *comedor* has the migrants sign the checks over to him. He then crosses the border back into Arizona to cash the checks, returning to *el comedor* to distribute the money. Some of these checks are meager pay for work done while the migrant was in prison, usually issued by the Department of Corrections.

Kino is run and operated by the Jesuit Refugee Service and the Missionary Sisters of the Eucharist, staffed by dedicated volunteers. Two home-cooked meals are provided daily, as well as the distribution of clothing and personal care items. Prior to serving their guest a meal, the Sisters attempt to raise consciousness by making a presentation to the migrants concerning human rights violations due to U.S. immigration policies. The day I visited the *comedor*, servers brought tortillas and salsa, plates of beans, rice, along with some chicken mole to the long wooden tables with benches. The plates were passed until everyone had one. The cafeteria line is intentionally avoided to create the atmosphere of eating in someone's home, providing these returning migrants some sense of dignity after the humiliations faced while in the United States. Because many of the deportees arrive with severely blistered feet, flu symptoms, and dehydration, a first-aid clinic is set up.

Across the street is the Nazareth House, a shelter for migrant women and children, who like Ms. Lopez are vulnerable on the streets of Nogales. While visiting Nazareth House, Sister Rosalba Avalos Ramos tells me that she often

21. Kino Border Initiative Annual Report 2014.

encounters women with feelings of helplessness, impotence, sadness, and indignation due to the injustices and abuse that they face and experience. "Generally, women arrive with a very painful story," Sister Avalos Ramos tells me. "These migrant women arrive at our shelter, without hope, with their hearts destroyed by suffering, despair, fear, and sadness. Some have been abandoned by their husbands and have the responsibility of taking care of three or four children. And in the midst of that struggle and that pain the women are faced with the reality of having to migrate." These ministries are replicated in other border cities, from Tijuana to Matamoros.

Unaware of these services, Ms. Lopez wandered the streets staying close to the border, as if that infernal wall which snakes across the landscape could provide some sense of security. Still, the wall was the closest she could get to home. That first night, and other subsequent nights, she cried herself to sleep in an empty cargo car by the train tracks close to the wall. Living on the streets homeless, she was unable to receive any assistance, not knowing where to go because she had no family in the country, nor knowing what to do because she lacked Spanish skills, nor any way to earn money because she had no identifications by which to gain employment. It appeared as if prostitution was her only option. Her last night in Mexico, she decided to use her precious cash to pay for a room at a fleabag motel. That night she noticed through her window some *mafiosos* pulling up to the hotel with girls younger then herself, some which seem to be preadolescence—all appeared to be drugged by the way they staggered. Through the thin walls she could hear these girls scream for help as they were being abused. She barely slept that night fearful the men would break down her own door and assault her.

The next day she left penniless to again wander the streets. A week had gone by and this frightened teenager was growing desperate. As she left the motel, a tall strange man started following her toward the train tracks. She was accosted with a knife, as he grabbed her from behind. She broke loose and ran for her life. She ran towards home, towards her salvation, toward the north. As fast as she could, she ran up the vehicle lanes of the DeConcini Port of Entry, running and screaming for help, seeking asylum. U.S. border officials captured and detained her, promising an asylum officer would soon speak to her concerning her ordeal in Mexico. Instead she was charged with a felony for illegal re-entry after a deportation, violating the protocols established for asylum seekers. She was transferred to a for-profit prison in Florence, Arizona for four months. Afterwards, she was transferred back to Eloy Detention Center where she spent the next two years fighting for asylum. Re-entry without proper documentation carries a maximum penalty of ten years in prison and/or a $250,000 fine with two to three years of probation.

Since her arrest in 2011, Ms. Lopez has spent almost three years in prison not only fighting her immigration case, but in a sense, fighting for her life. The flower of her youth spent behind bars due to a broken immigration system. She endured constant humiliations. She was forced on numerous occasions to strip and experience cavity searches. She was constantly taunted and threatened by the guards who would call her a little bitch, along with more colorful terms. They would shackle her by the ankles, waist, and wrists from 11 pm until the next day whenever she had a court hearing, only uncuffing one hand so she could use the bathroom. The irony is that due to the Deferred Action for Childhood Arrivals program none of this needed to occur if it wasn't for the felony of illegal re-entry. But she didn't illegally reenter the U.S.—she sought asylum, fearing for her life.

She was released on a $6,000 bail in November 2013, about a month before we sat down and I heard her story. Hearing her ordeal, I was cognizant that my own daughter, whose father at one time was also undocumented, is the same age as Sandra. Ms. Lopez recounted the story of a fellow twenty-two-year-old inmate who after a month at Eloy couldn't take it anymore and hung herself. I asked Ms. Lopez what kept her going. Her face lit up as she began to tell me how three years of constant prayers provided the serenity, the presence of God, to endure constant degradations. "What doesn't kill you," she reminded me, "makes you stronger." No young person who grew up in this country, whose parents pay taxes, regardless of their faith tradition (or lack thereof) should undergo what Ms. Lopez has suffered. Unfortunately, Ms. Lopez is but one story among millions of lives being broken by our immigration policies. No question she has paid a heavy price, but woe to those of us who continue to ignore the great human violation that continues to occur today in this country, on our southern borders.

Ironically, many who support family values have created the very laws that have torn Ms. Lopez as a teenage girl from her own family. Ironically, those centering their faith on the importance of maintaining and sustaining the integrity of the family remain silent as Latinx fathers and mothers are separated from their children and deported. Ironically, those who build walls to protect their families from menace of Latinxs contribute to Latinx men leaving their own families south of the border to come work so as to provide money for loved ones back home. But with the passage of time, unable to cross the wall that was built and too dangerous to return if they do visit home, they find themselves eventually ending those relationships due to prolong separation, starting new relationships here.

Ms. Lopez ends her conversation proclaiming, "I'm more mature, stronger, I felt like I had no one, but I lacked nothing cause I had God. . . . Now I'm free, thank God, I am free."

Three years have passed since we first spoke. At twenty-five, Ms. Lopez, under a temporary stay while her case was being reviewed, enrolled at Maricopa Community College. Her drug conviction was reduced to a misdemeanor. And while it is tempting to say that all works for good for those who are called according to God's purposes, I remain cognizant that Ms. Lopez's ordeal is yet to be over. As this book goes to press, I discovered that the Board of Immigration Appeal issued a final order of removal. This means that at any moment, Ms. Lopez can be detained and removed from the United States. When she re-entered the United States seeking asylum, she was charged with a felony for unlawful reentry. This felony prevents her from becoming a DACA Dreamer.

Her only hope is for the U.S. Supreme Court to uphold President Obama's November 20, 2014 Executive Order known as the Deferred Acton for Childhood Arrivals or DACA II. In light of Congressional inaction, the Administrative branch of government attempted to provide some reform to the current broken immigration system. If DACA II goes into effect, Ms. Lopez's reentry conviction would not preclude her application for Dreamer status. DACA II was set to take affect on February 2016; however, a lawsuit was filed to halt the Executive Order in December 2015 resulting in a temporary injunction (freeze) as a federal judge considered DACA II's legality. The Obama Administration appealed the injunction which the Fifth circuit upheld. Currently the case is before the U.S. Supreme Court with a decision expected in the summer of 2016, after this book is published. If the Supreme Court rules in favor of the Obama Administration, Ms. Lopez can apply under the provisions of DACA II and stay in the only home she has ever known. If not, then she may need to obtain sanctuary in a house of worship.

DISCUSSION QUESTIONS

- Should those who came as baby/children be deported if they lack documentation? Should they be able to attend public schools, college, drive a car, work? Is DACA good? Why or why not?

- What role do CCA and GEO play in the judicial process? Should pro-profit prisons exist? Why or why not? What hazards does the undocumented face when incarcerated? What conflicts, if any, arise between pro-profit prisons and the judicial system? Or the state/federal legislature? How cost effective are pro-profit prisons?

- Is our current deportation process humane? Why or why not? Should women and children be deported in the middle of the night to dangerous border towns? Why or why not? What hazards does the deportee face? Is this an effective example of "deterrence"?

Conclusion

AGAINST HOSPITALITY

THE GOVERNMENT'S AFFIDAVIT WAS dated June 21, 1960. At the time I was occupying a one-room apartment in the slums of Manhattan with my parents, a roach, and rat infested four floor walk-up close to Hell's Kitchen, sharing one bathroom with the other tenants on the floor. We arrived in this country with a tourist visa on April Fool's Day, 1960. As a toddler, I was unable to understand the letter's importance; nonetheless, this binding legal document constructed my identity in the eyes of the dominant U.S. culture. Citing Section 242 of the Immigration and Nationality Act, the letter placed me on notice that deportation procedures were imminent. I was ordered to voluntarily "self deport" in lieu of forced expatriation. The moment I received this affidavit, I became an undocumented immigrant, what some today insist on derogatorily calling an "illegal alien." Ironically, I found myself in the same country directly responsible for the exile from my homeland. And when I eventually die, I am fully aware that my bones will be interred in this foreign soil, a land that has never embraced me as one of its own, regardless of the decades of contributing to its welfare. My family's presence in this country was not originally based on some desire for liberty or pursuit of economic opportunities; we were in this alien land as a direct result of U.S. foreign policies that deprived my country of origin, Cuba, of political and economic sovereignty during the first half of the twentieth century. If truth be told, I would have preferred to live in my own country, among my own people, rooted in my own culture.

The irony of our current U.S. immigration debate, a paradox conveniently ignored by politicians and unknown to most citizens, is that U.S. foreign policies are directly responsible for the growing Latinx presence in this country. Nevertheless, we convince ourselves that they are coming with their anchor babies to take away our jobs and use up all of our generous social services. Or, more benignly, they are coming in search of the American Dream hoping to find a better life for themselves and their families. These are the two most common answers given when asked why "they" cross the border; but both narratives are erroneous.

Photographer: Vincent De La Torre

The reality is that most, like myself, would rather remain in their homeland, but instead are forced to leave for the insecurity of border crossing because the U.S. created political and economic uncertainty in their country due to a foreign policy designed to secure the avarice of multinational corporations. The United States will never be able to rectify, in a justice-based matter, its complicity in creating our current immigration crisis until it is able to understand why "they" came and why "they" continue to come. After reading this book, I hope that a more complex and nuanced comprehension of our current immigration predicament now exists in the mind of the reader. The hope was that by joining me in occupying the physical spaces where the cries of migrants are heard, the consciousness of the reader was raised beyond nonsensical anti-immigrant rhetoric.

We have seen how harline politicians, attempting to garner votes, inveigh against foreigners, presenting the undocumented as a threat to U.S. security and a danger to everyday "real" Americans. It would be wrong to conclude that the prevailing anti-migrant rhetoric is the exceptional extreme to the current immigration discourse. Quite the contrary, it is the norm of a neo-nativist attitude that has lead the nation to previously unimaginable depths of vitriolic bigotry. During the 2016 presidential elections, Republican candidates—speaking to their base—have engaged in a one-upmanship of outdoing their opponents by proposing greater life-threatening intolerance to the cheers of approving crowds. All advocate weaponized drones targeting border crossers, constructing a 2,000-mile fence stretching from the Pacific to the Gulf, and building more private prisons to accompany the entire family (including babies and children).

The most disturbing proposition is the creation of a modern day Trail of Tears through the mass deportation of over eleven million undocumented Latinxs. Even the U.S. Immigration and Customs Enforcement Agency estimates that deporting all eleven million undocumented persons would cost $8,318 per person.[1] According to UCLA professor Raúl Hinojosa-Ojeda, eleven million immigrants would be the equivalent to more than $1.5 trillion (roughly one percent), added to the gross domestic product (GDP) during a ten-year period. Mass deportation, on the other hand, will reduce the GDP by $2.6 trillion annually (1.46 percent) over ten years, not including the 91.5 trillion in actual cost of deportation. And while wages would rise for less-skilled U.S. workers, there would be a decline for higher skilled U.S. workers, leading to widespread job loss.[2] Economics 101 teaches us that moving more people to legal employment creates more opportunities for money to circulate, adding, according to one report, a cumulative $470 billion increase of personal income for all Americans over a ten year period.[3] But, Latinxphobia trumps fiscal responsibility. These police-state solution, normative to a vast majority of right-wing politicians and their constituents, has become the acceptable anti-Latinx rhetoric, and will remain long after the 2016 presidential campaigns comes to a close.

That conservative-leaning politicians are specifically hostile to Latinx immigration, and Latinxs in general, should not be surprising to the reader of this book. So, for the concluding remarks, I should rather not rehash such blatant racism coming from the more conservative on the political spectrum and instead focus on the problematic rhetoric more normatively expressed by liberals. Common justification for progressive views expressed on immigration emanate among many political and especially religious liberals in the rhetoric of hospitality. The virtue

1. Ordoñez, "Immigration Reform."

2. Hinojosa-Ojeda, "Economic Benefits," 176–77.

3. Lynch and Oakford, "National and State-by-State Economic Benefits," 2.

of hospitality becomes our religious or civic duty to assist (bring salvation to) these poor unfortunate souls, for after all, there go I but by the grace of God. For example, 2016 Democratic presidential candidate, Martin O'Malley, approached immigration by stating, "We are not a country that should send children away and send them back to certain death." He called "hospitality to strangers" an "essential human dignity."[4]

Hospitality is a biblical concept that means more than just opening one's home to the stranger and inviting them for a meal. The God described in the Hebrew Bible consistently reminds the Jews not to forget the story of Abram the alien, or their time in Egypt as slaves; and thus, be just to the sojourner residing among you. The New Testament reminds us to show hospitality to strangers, for in so doing, some have shown hospitality to angels without realizing (Heb 13:2). The biblical term "stranger" or "sojourner" best captures the predicament of the today's undocumented. This term connotes the in-between space of neither being native-born nor a foreigner. As such, the alien lacks the benefits and protection ordinarily provided to those tied to the land due to their birthplace. Vulnerable to those who profit from their labor, the alien derives security from the biblical mandate of hospitality. Treatment of the alien is based on three biblical presuppositions: 1) the Jews were once aliens who were oppressed by the natives of the land of Egypt (Exod 22:21); 2) God always sides and intervenes to liberate the disenfranchised (Exod 23:9); and 3) God's covenant with Israel is contingent on all members of the community benefitting, regardless if they are Jewish or not (Deut 26:11).

Those who read the New Testament discover that the authors of the gospels connect the alien with the hope of

4. Hing, "Who Would Win."

salvation. "And . . . an angel of the Lord appeared to Joseph in a dream, saying 'Rise up! Take the child and his mother with you and flee into Egypt, and stay there until I tell you, for Herod will look for the child in order to destroy him.' And rising up, he took the child and his mother that night and fled to Egypt" (Matt 2:13–14). While most who read this scriptural passage with the privilege of citizenship may not necessarily find these verses inspiring or profound, those of us who are or have been undocumented, read God's hope actively connecting with our hopelessness of being uprooted. Responsibility toward aliens is so paramount that God incarnated God's self as an alien. The radicalism of the incarnation for Christians is not so much that the Creator of the universe became a frail human, but rather that God chose to become undocumented, fleeing the oppressive consequences of the empire of the time. In so doing, Jesus willingly assumed the role of the ultra-disenfranchised. Over two thousand years ago the Holy family arrived in Egypt as political refugees, migrants fleeing the tyrannical regime of Herod, imposed upon the local population by distance colonial powers in Rome.

Jesus' physical presence in Egypt forces us to ask why he occupied that particular place. Herod's responsibility was to ensure profits, in the form of taxes, flowed to the Roman center with as little resistance as possible. Of course, he financially benefited from this relation, as do many elites within Latin American countries today who sign trade agreements that are disadvantageous to their compatriots. Jesus, a colonized man, was an undocumented alien, a victim of political circumstances beyond his comprehension or control. To ask why Jesus was in Egypt is to ask why Latinxs are in the United States.

As Rome benefited due to *pax romana*[5] brought about by territorial expansion, Americans benefitted by the ninetieth century jingoist religious ideology of Manifest Destiny that justified Anglo territorial expansion in North America. The massive land acquisitions of northern Mexico, as we have seen in this book, was based on a theology that conceived the dominant Euroamerican culture as chosen by God who destined Euroamericans to acquire the entire continent. The expansionist war against Mexico was minimized by the false creation of the U.S.'s historical metanarrative that masked the fact that it was the economic borders of empire that crossed the Western Hemisphere—not the other way around.

More important than territorial expansion, was the U.S. attempt to control the economies of other nations. While empires of old, like Rome, relied on brute force, the U.S. Empire relies mainly on economic force (not to disregard the fact that it also has the largest military apparatus ever known to humanity). Through its economic might, the United States dictates terms of trade with other nations, guaranteeing that benefits flow to the U.S. center and the elites from the countries that agreed to the trade agreements. This strategy became a neoliberal based foreign policy during the twentieth century that moved the focus from acquiring the lands of others toward a hegemonic control of the economies of others. The political situation brought about by colonization during the time of Jesus, pushed his family, out of fear for their lives, toward Egypt.

Because Jesus was not the first biblical character to experience alienation as an immigrant, many faith institutions, like the Catholic Church, provide guidelines on how to treat the alien within our midst. In the encyclical *Gaudium et Spes*, the church writes:

5. Latin for "the Roman peace"

> Justice and equity likewise require that the mo-
> bility which is necessary in a developing econo-
> my be regulated in such a way as to keep the life
> of individuals and their families from becoming
> insecure and precarious. Hence, when workers
> come from another country or district and con-
> tribute by their labor to the economic advance-
> ment of a nation or region, all discrimination
> with respect to wages and working conditions
> must be carefully avoided.[6]

God chooses the oppressed of history—the hungry, the thirsty, the naked, the alien, the sick, the prisoner—and makes them the cornerstone, the principal means for salvation. In fact, whatsoever we do to these, the very least among us—we do it unto Jesus. And because the undocumented crossing the borders are usually the hungry, the thirsty, the naked, and of course the alien; because they are often the sick due to the hazards of their journey, and when caught by the Border Patrol become the prisoner; if we want to see the face of Jesus, all we need to do is gaze into the face of the undocumented. God does not appear to the Pharaohs or Caesars or Prime Ministers or Presidents of history. Leaders of empires whose policies cause death and migration are more aligned with the satanic than with the divine. For this reason, God appears as and to their slaves, their vassals, and those alienated by their empires. Among the disenfranchised of the land are the undocumented, be they Jesus in the past or Jesús the Central American crossing the border today.

For many from the dominant culture who have a more liberal interpretation to the biblical text, hospitality undergirds how they approach and treat the undocumented. While it may be desirable for all to participate in this virtue,

6. Second Vatican Council, *Gaudium et Spes*, 1.66.

caution needs to be taken that the practice of hospitality does not mask deep-rooted injustices. For some liberals and leftists, the proper response toward today's undocumented aliens is to demonstrate the virtue of hospitality. Yet, the virtue of hospitality, I argue, is not the best way to approach our current immigration crisis. Throughout this book we have considered the consequences of implementing in 1994 the North American Free Trade Agreement (NAFTA). We explored the nineteenth century policy of Manifest Destiny that deprived Mexico of half its northern territory. We considered how the twentieth century policy of Gun Boat Diplomacy unleashed a colonial venture that deprived Central American countries of their natural resources while providing the U.S. with an unlimited supply of cheap labor. Also, we examined the inhumanity of Operation Gatekeeper and Streamline.

The undocumented attempt the hazardous crossing because our foreign and trade policies from the nineteenth through the twentieth-first century has created an economic situation in their countries where they are unable to feed their families. A major thesis of this book has maintained that when the U.S. military, for over a century, provided the freedom for U.S. corporations (i.e., the United Fruit Company) to build roads into developing Latin American countries to extract, by brute force if necessary, their natural resources; many of the inhabitants of those same countries, myself included, deprived of a livelihood, take those same roads following their resources. I am in this country following my sugar, tobacco, and rum.

The U.S. has a Latin American immigration crisis, yet a failure exists in recognizing that the reason they come is because they are following what has been stolen from them. They come to escape the violence and terror that the U.S. historically unleashed upon them in an effort to protect *paxamericana*, a needed status quo if American foreign business interests are to flourish. An immigration problem exists because, for over a century and a half, the U.S. has exploited—and continues to exploit via NAFTA—their neighbors to the south.

To practice the virtue of hospitality assumes the "house" belongs to the one practicing this virtue who, out of the generosity of their heart, is sharing her or his resources with the Other who has no claim to the possession. But it was due to Latin American natural resources and cheap labor that the U.S. house was built in the first place. The virtue of hospitality masks the complexity caused by the consequences of empire building. Due to U.S. sponsored "banana republics" throughout the nineteenth and twentieth century, Latin Americans holds a lien on this U.S. house's title. Rather than speaking about the virtue of hospitality, it would historically be more accurate to speak about the responsibility of restitution.[7] Maybe the ethical question we should be asking is not "why" are they coming, but how do we begin to make reparations for all we have stolen to create the present economic empire we call the United States?

DISCUSSION QUESTIONS

- Why reject hospitality? How does hospitality mask complicity? What would restitution look like?

- How feasible and cost affective is it to deport everyone? What are the obstacles faced in mass deportation? Or of building a wall along the entire southern border? If these are unattainable actions, why do politicians continue to advance such propositions?

7. De La Torre, *Trails of Hope and Terror*, 9–14.

- What religious considerations should inform the current immigration discussion? Can one be anti-immigrant and a Christian? Why or why not?

BIBLIOGRAPHY

Aguirre, Eduardo. "Deaths in the Desert." Kino Border Initiative. July 7, 2015. Online: https://www.kinoborderinitiative.org/deaths-in-the-desert/.

Ahlstrom, Sydney E. *A Religious History of the American People.* New Haven, CT: Yale University Press, 1972.

American Civil Liberties Union. *Creating the Minutemen: A Small Extremist Group's Campaign Fueled by Misinformation.* April 2006. Online: http://www.ilw.com/articles/2006,0619-ybarra.pdf.

Andrews, Edmund L. "Rich Nations Criticized for Barriers to Trade." *The New York Times.* September 30, 2002.

Anzaldúa, Gloria E. *Borderlands/La Frontera: The New Mestiza.* San Francisco: Spinsters/Aunt Lute, 1987.

Archibold, Randal C. "Government Issues Waiver for Fencing Along Border." *The New York Times.* April 2, 2008.

"Arizona Protesters Mistake Busload of YMCA campers for Immigrant Children." *CBS News.* July 16, 2014.

Bailey, Phillip M. "Prosecutor Slammed for Hispanic Bias Comment." *The Louisville Courier-Journal.* October 15, 2015.

Barlett, Donald L., and James B. Steele. *The Betrayal of the American Dream.* New York: Public Affairs, 2012.

Barrionuevo, Alexei. "Mountains of Corn and a Sea of Farm Subsidies." *The New York Times.* November 9, 2005.

Bazelon, Emily. "The Unwelcome Return of 'Illegals.'" *The New York Times Magazine.* August 18, 2015.

Becker, Andrew. "Lawmaker Calls for New Investigations into Border Agent Fatal Shootings." *Center for Investigative Reporting.* September 12, 2014.

Becker, Elizabeth. "Western Farmers Fear Third-World Challenge to Subsidies." *The New York Times*. September 9, 2003.

Bello, Walden. "The World Bank, the IMF, and the Multinationals: Manufacturing the World Food Crises." *The Nation*. June 8, 2008.

Bennett, Brian. "Border Patrol's Use of Deadly Force Criticized in Report." *Los Angeles Times*. February 27, 2014.

Bryce, Robert. "The Ethanol Scam: Burning Food to Make Motor Fuel." In *Food, Inc.*, edited by Karl Weber, 91–93. New York: Public Affairs, 2009.

Center for Latin American Studies. *In the Shadow of the Wall: Family Separation, Immigration Enforcement and Security*. Tucson: Arizona University, 2013.

Cohen, Michael. "How For-Profit Prisons Have Become the Biggest Lobby No One Is Talking About." *The Washington Post*. April 28, 2015.

Corbett, Jim. *The Sanctuary Church*. Wallingford, PA: Pendle Hill, 1986.

Curry, Bill. "8 of 11 Activists Guilty in Alien Sanctuary Case: Defiant Group Says 6-Month Trail Hasn't Ended Movement to Help Central American Refugees." *Los Angeles Times*. May 2, 1986.

Dale, Mariana. "Babeu Keeps Peace but Buses with Migrants Kids a No-Show." *The Republic*. July 15, 2014.

De La Torre, Miguel A. *Trails of Hope and Terror: Testimonies on Immigration*. Maryknoll, NY: Orbis, 2009.

Delgado, Richard. "The Law of the Noose: A History of Latino Lynching." *Harvard Civil Rights-Civil Liberties Law Review* 44 (2009) 298–302.

Delgado Wise, Raúl, and Humberto Márquez Covarrubias. "Capitalist Restructuring, Development and the Labour Migration: The Mexico-U.S. Case." *Third World Quarterly* 29.7 (2008) 1372.

Department of Justice. *National Drug Threat Assessment 2011*. Washington DC: Department of Justice, 2011.

Detention Watch Network. *About the U.S. Detention and Deportation System*. Washington DC: Detention Watch Network, 2012.

DiNatale, Sara, and Maria Sacchetti. "South Boston Brothers Allegedly Beat Homeless Man." *Boston Globe*. August 19, 2015.

Dugger, Celia. "Report Finds Few Benefits for Mexico in NAFTA." *The New York Times*. November 19, 2003.

Fears, Darryl. "3 Jailed Immigrants Die in a Month." *The Washington Post*. August 15, 2007.

Fernandez, Manny. "Immigrants Fight Texas' Birth Certificate Rules." *The New York Times*. September 17, 2015.

————. "Teenager Testifies About Attacking Latinos for Sport." *The New York Times*. March 29, 2010.

Fife, John. "New Sanctuary Movement at the Border Can Spiritually Transform Us." *National Catholic Reporter*. July 6, 2012.

Fisher, Michael J. "Use of Safe Tactics and Techniques." *U.S. Customs and Border Protection Memo*. March 7, 2014.

Fitting, Elizabeth. *The Struggle for Maize: Campesinos, Workers, and Transgenic Corn in the Mexican Countryside*. Durham, NC: Duke University Press, 2011.

Floyd-Thomas, Stacey. *Deeper Shades of Purple: Womanism in Religion and Society*. New York: New York University Press, 2006.

Gardner, Matthew, Sebastian Johnson, and Meg Wiehe. *Undocumented Immigrant State & Local Tax Contributions. Institute on Taxation & Economic Policy*. April 2015.

Geertz, Clifford. *The Interpretations of Culture: Selected Essays*. New York: Basic, 1973.

Godoy, Emilio. "Mexico: Maquiladora Factories Toxic Pollutants." *Inter Press Service*. August 23, 2011.

Golden, Renny, and Michael McConnell. *Sanctuary: The New Underground Railroad*. Maryknoll, NY: Orbis, 1986.

Government Accounting Office. "Border Patrol: Costs and Challenges Related to Training New Agents." GAO-07-997T. June 19, 2007.

————. "Secure Border Initiative, DHS Has Faced Challenges Deploying Technology and Fencing Along the Southwest Border." May 4, 2010.

Graff, Garrett M. "The Green Monster: How the Border Patrol became America's Most Out-of-Control Law Enforcement Agency." *Politico Magazine*. November/December 2014.

Greenhouse, Steven. "City Feels Early Effects of Plant Closing in 2004." *The New York Times*. December 26, 2002.

Gzesh, Susan. "Central Americans and Asylum Policy in the Reagan Era." *Migration Policy Institute*. April 1, 2006.

Harris, Elise. "Pope Denounces 'Racist, Xenophobic' Attitudes Toward Immigrants." *Catholic News Agency*. July 15, 2014.

Harris, Gardiner. "Obama, in Call for Reform, Defends the Black Lives Matter Movement." *The New York Times*. October 23, 2015.

Holstege, Sean, and Mariana Dale. "Protestors in Oracle Inspired by Murrieta." *The Republic*. July 14, 2014.

Holthouse, David. "Arizona Showdown: High-powered Firearms, Militia Maneuvers and Racism at the Minuteman Project." *Intelligence Report* 118 (Summer 2005).

Hing, Julianne. "Who Would Win an Immigration Debate Between Sanders and Clinton? Martin O'Malley." *The Nation.* November 3, 2015.

Hinojosa-Ojeda, Raúl. "The Economic Benefits of Comprehensive Immigration Reform." *Cato Journal* 32.1 (2012) 176–77.

ICE Newsroom. "ICE Detainee Passes Away at Eloy Detention Center." May 21, 2015. Online: https://www.ice.gov/news/releases/ice-detainee-passes-away-eloy-detention-facility.

"Immigration Non-Harvest." *The Wall Street Journal.* July 20, 2007.

Immigration Policy Center. *Immigrants and Crime: Are they Connected?: Immigration Fact-Check.* Washington, DC: Immigration Policy Center, 2008.

Jackson, Robert H. *The Nuremberg Case as Presented by Robert H. Jackson.* New York: Cooper Square, 1971.

Jenkins, Virginia Scott. *Bananas: The American History.* Washington, DC: Smithsonian Institution, 2000.

Jimenez, Maria. *Humanitarian Crises: Migrant Deaths at the U.S.— Mexico Border.* San Diego: ACLU of San Diego and Imperial Counties with Mexico's National Human Rights Commission, October, 2009.

Kino Border Initiative. Annual Report, 2014. Online: https://www.kinoborderinitiative.org/wp-content/uploads/2013/09/KBI_AnnualReport_2014_FINAL_forweb.pdf.

Labor Council for Latin American Advancement (LCLAA). *Another America Is Possible: The Impact of NAFTA on the U.S. Latino Community and Lessons for Future Trade Agreements,* Product ID 9013. Washington, DC: Public Citizen's Global Trade Watch, 2004.

Lacey, Marc. "Border Deployment Will Take Weeks." *The New York Times.* August 1, 2010.

Laughland, Oliver. "Justice Department Asks Judge to Leave Migrant Families in Detention Centers." *The Guardian.* August 7, 2015.

Lemons, Stephen. "Former Minuteman Leader Chris Simcox Can Cross-Examine One Child Victim Face-to-Face, Judge Rules." *The Phoenix Times.* August 21, 2015.

Light, Michael T., Mark Hugo Lopez, and Ana Gonzalez-Barrera, "The Rise of Federal Immigration Crimes: Unlawful Reentry Drives Growth." *Pew Research Center.* March 18, 2014.

LoMonaco, Claudine. "Many Border Deaths Unlisted." *Tucson Citizen.* June, 30, 2003.

López, Ann Aurelia. *The Farmworkers' Journal.* Berkeley: University of California Press, 2007.

Bibliography

Lydgate, Loanna. *Assembly-Line Justice: A Review of Operations Streamline*. Berkeley, CA: University of California, 2010.

Lynch, Robert, and Patrick Oakford. "National and State-by-State Economic Benefits of Immigration Reform." Report from the Center for American Progress. May 17, 2013.

Massey, Douglas S. "Foreword." In *Latinas/os in the United States: Changing the Face of América*, edited by Havidán Rodríguez, Rogelio Sáenz, and Cecilia Menjívar. New York: Springer, 2008.

McCombs, Brandy. "Abuse Tales Hard to Dispel." *Arizona Daily Star*. October 19, 2008.

McDonnell, Patrick J. "Official Says Border Killing Victim Might Have Lived." *Los Angeles Times*. June 20, 1992.

McElwee, Joshua J. "Francis Cries Out for Welcoming Church." *National Catholic Reporter*. November 18, 2015.

McIntire Peters, Katherine. "Up Against the Wall." *Government Executive*. October 1, 1996. Online: http://www.govexec.com/archdoc/1096/1096s1.htm.

McKinley Jr, James C. "Mexican Farmers Protest End of Corn-Import Taxes." *The New York Times*. February 1, 2008.

McLean, Dan. "Immigration's Tancredo's Top Topics." *New Hampshire Sunday News*. June 12, 2005.

"Mexicans Deported from U.S. Face Shattered Lives." *The Associated Press*. August 25, 2008.

Millis, Dan. "Testimony from a Border Activist." In *Trails of Hope and Terror: Testimonies on Immigration*, edited by Miguel A. De La Torre, 21–25. Maryknoll, NY: Orbis, 2009.

Mitchell, Donald. "A Note on Rising Food Prices." Policy Research Working Paper #4682. World Bank Development Prospects Group. April, 2008.

"Modes of Entry for the Unauthorized Migrant Population." *Pew Hispanic Center Fact Sheet*. May 22, 2006. Online: http://www.pewhispanic.org/files/2011/10/19.pdf.

Montes, Juan. "Mexico Looks to Raise Wages." *The Wall Street Journal*. August 28, 2014.

Moore, Solomon. "Push on Immigration Crimes Is Said to Shift Focus." *The New York Times*. January 11, 2009.

———. "Study Shows Sharp Rise in Latino Federal Convicts." *The New York Times*. February 18, 2009.

"NAFTA at 20: Ready to Take Off Again?" *The Economist*. January 4, 2014.

Nelson-Pallmeyer, Jack. *School of Assassins: Guns, Greed, and Globalization*. Maryknoll, NY: Orbis, 2001.

Nevins, Joseph. "How High Must Operation Gatekeeper's Death Count Go?" *Los Angeles Times*. November 19, 2000.

———. "Border Patrol Agent Charged in Murder Is Linked to Drug Theft." *Los Angeles Times*. July 24, 1992.

No More Deaths. *A Culture of Cruelty: Abuse and Impunity in Short-Term U.S. Border Patrol Custody.* Tucson, AZ: No More Deaths, 2011.

———. *Crossing the Line: Human Rights Abuses of Migrants in Short-Term Custody on the Arizona/Sonora Border.* Tucson, AZ: No More Deaths, 2008.

Office of Inspector General. *Streamline: Measure Its Effect on Illegal Border Crossing.* Washington, DC: Department of Homeland Security, 2015.

Ogren, Cassandra. "Migration and Human Rights on the Mexico-Guatemala Border." *International Migration* 45.4 (2007) 226.

Oppel, Jr, Richard A. "Private Prisons Found to Offer Little in Savings." *The New York Times*. May 18, 2011.

Ordoñez, Silvana. "Immigration Reform: Good or Bad for the Economy?" *NBC*. February 2, 2013.

Ortega, Bob, and Rob O'Dell. "Deadly Border Agent Incidents Cloaked in Silence." *The Arizona Republic*. December 16, 2013.

Ortiz, Ildefonso. "Agent Sexually Assaults Family, Kidnaps Girl, Commits Suicide." *The Brownsville Herald*. March 13, 2014.

O'Sullivan, John. "Annexation." *United States Magazine and Democratic Review* 17.1 (1845) 5.

Parker, Ryan. "Minutemen Project Beginning Recruiting Volunteers to Man U.S. Border." *The Los Angeles Times*. July 10, 2014.

Police Executive Research Forum. *Use of Force Review: Cases and Policies.* Washington, DC: U.S. Customs and Border Protection, 2013.

Regan, Margaret. *The Death of Josseline: Immigration Stories from the Arizona Borderlands.* Boston: Beacon, 2010.

Reuters. "Mexico Poverty Rate Hit 46.2 Percent Last Year as 2 Million More Join Ranks of Poor." *Japan Times*. July, 24, 2015.

Robertson, Alistair Graham, et al. *Operation Streamline: Costs and Consequences.* Charlotte, NC: Grassroots Leadership, September 2012.

Rocca, Francis X. "Pope Drancis Calls On Europe's Catholics to Shelter Refugees." *The Wall Street Journal*. September 6, 2015.

Rosenberg, Tina. "The Free-Trade Fix." *The New York Times Magazine*. August 18, 2002.

————. "Why Mexico's Small Corn Farmers Go Hungry." *The New York Times.* March 3, 2003.

Rotella, Sebastian. "Ex-Border Patrol Agent Acquitted in 1992 Slaying." *Los Angeles Times.* Feburary 4, 1994.

Rubio-Goldsmith, et al. *"Funnel Effect" and Recovered Bodies of Unauthorized Migrants Processed by the Pima County Office of the Medical Examiner, 1990–2005.* Tucson: BMI, 2006.

Sakuma, Amanda. "Undocumented Workers are Keeping a Key Benefit Program Afloat." *MSNBC.* August 12, 2014.

Santos, Fernanda. "Detainees Sentenced in Seconds in Streamline Justice on Border." *The New York Times.* February 11, 2014.

Santos, Fernanda, and Rebekah Zemansky, "Arizona Desert Swallows Migrants on Riskier Trails." *The New York Times.* May 20, 2013.

Schiavocampo, Mara. "Anti-Latino Hate Crimes." *NBC Nightly News.* September 2, 2009.

School of Assassins. Maryknoll World Productions. New York: Films Media Group, 1995.

Scott, Robert E., et al. "Revisiting NAFTA: Still Not Working for North." Briefing Paper #173 Washington DC: Economic Policy Institute, 2006.

Sergie, Mohammed Aly. "NAFTA's Economic Impact." Annual Council on Foreign Relations. February 14, 2014.

Shah, Silky, et al. *Banking on Detention: Local Lockup Quotas & the Immigration Dragnet.* Washington, DC: Detention Watch Network, 2015.

Sheldon, Hailey Anne. "Operation Streamline: The Border Patrol Prosecution Initiative." *The Public Purpose* 11 (2013) 92.

Sherman, Rachel Ewing. "Catholic Mission." *Catholic World* 40.235 (1885) 106.

Shulz, G. W. "More High-Tech Setback for Border Security." *Politics Daily.* May 23, 2010.

Slack, Jeremy, et al. *In the Shadow of the Wall: Family Separation, Immigration Enforcement and Security.* Tucson, AZ: University of Arizona, 2013.

Smith, Robert F. *What Happened in Cuba? A Documentary History.* New York: Twayne, 1963.

Stana, Richard M. *INS Southwest Border Strategy: Resource and Impact Issues Remain After Seven Years.* Washington, DC: U.S. General Accounting Office, 2001.

Steinhaur, Jennifer. "Bipartisan Push Builds to Relax Sentencing Laws." *The New York Times.* July 28, 2015.

Striffler, Steve, and Mark Moberg, eds. *Banana Wars: Power, Production, and History in the Americas.* Durham, NC: Duke University, 2003.

Takaki, Ronald. *A Different Mirror: A History of Multicultural America.* Boston: Little, Brown and Company, 1993.

Tartaglia, Mike. "Private Prisons, Private Records." *Boston University Law Review* 94.5 (2014) 1695–96.

Thandeka. *Learning to be White: Money, Race, and God in America.* New York: Continuum, 1999.

Transaction Records Access Clearinghouse. "FY 2009 Federal Prosecutions Sharply Higher." *Syracuse University.* December 1, 2009.

———. "Arizona Federal Prosecutions Driven to Record Highs." *Syracuse University.* August 17, 2010.

Trevizo, Perla. "Operation Streamline Takes Hard Line on Illegal Border Crossers." *Arizona Daily Star.* March 24, 2013.

U.S. Department of Justice Office of the Inspector General. "Inspection of the Influx of New Personnel." Online: http://www.usdoj.gov/oig/reports/INS/e0018/exec.htm.

U.S. General Accounting Office. "Illegal Immigration: Border-crossing Deaths have Doubled since 1995; Border Patrol's Efforts to Prevent Deaths have not been Fully Evaluated." GAO-05–435 (2006).

———. "North American Free Trade Agreement: Assessment of Major Issues." GAO/GGD–93–137 (1993).

U.S. Sentencing Commission. *Illegal Reentry Offences.* Washington, DC: United States Sentencing Commission, 2015.

"U.S. Will Have Minority White Sooner, Says Demographer." *National Public Radio.* June 27, 2011.

Villarreal, M. Angeles, and Ian F. Fergusson. "The North American Free Trade Agreement—NAFTA." *Congressional Research Service* (2015) ii.

Wilson, Christopher. *Crime Data and Spillover Violence along the Southwest Border.* Washington, DC: Woodrow Wilson International Center for Scholars, 2011.

Whitneck, Harris. "Mexican Farmers Protest NAFTA." *CNN.* February 1, 2008.

Ye Hee Lee, Michelle. "Donald Trump's False Comments Connecting Mexican Immigrants and Crime." *Washington Post.* July 8, 2015.

INDEX

Index

9 781498 223690